T0318453

The World of *Mister Rogers' Neighborhood*

Unlike many children's television shows, *Mister Rogers' Neighborhood* did more than simply entertain or occupy children's attention. The show educated them in the affective domain, encouraging such things as appreciation for difference, collaboration, self-expression, and self-worth. It also introduced them to the areas of culture, art, and music through guests, trips, art objects and processes, and demonstrations, making these accessible and meaningful in a way that a child could understand. While the educational content of children's television programming has improved greatly since the late 1960s, no other children's program has ever attempted such a mix of high art, low art, folk art, industrial production, learning in the affective and social domains, and more, all with a whimsical sense of humor, insight, and a level of interconnected detail unmatched by any other children's television program. This book illuminates and examines the world of *Mister Rogers' Neighborhood* through world design, narrative, genre, form, content, authorship, reception, and more.

Mark J.P. Wolf is a Full Professor of the Communication Department at Concordia University, Wisconsin. His books include *Abstracting Reality*, *The Medium of the Video Game*, *Virtual Morality*, *The Video Game Explosion*, *Myst and Riven: The World of the D'ni*, *Before the Crash*, *Encyclopedia of Video Games*, *Building Imaginary Worlds*, *The LEGO Studies Reader*, and *Video Games Around the World*. With Bernard Perron, he is the co-editor of *The Video Game Theory Reader* 1 and 2, and the Landmark Video Game book series.

Imaginary Worlds

Each volume in the Imaginary Worlds book series addresses a specific imaginary world, examining it in the light of a variety of approaches, including transmedial studies, world design, narrative, genre, form, content, authorship and reception, and its context within the imaginary world tradition. Each volume covers a historically significant imaginary world (in all its manifestations), and collectively the books in this series will produce an intimate examination of the imaginary world tradition, through the concrete details of the famous and influential worlds that have set the course and changed the direction of subcreation as an activity.

The World of *Mister Rogers' Neighborhood*
Mark J.P. Wolf

Forthcoming:

The World of *The Walking Dead*: Transmedia Horror for the Digital Age
Matthew Freeman

The World of *Mister Rogers' Neighborhood*

Mark J. P. Wolf

Routledge
Taylor & Francis Group

LONDON AND NEW YORK

First published 2017 by Routledge

2 Park Square, Milton Park, Abingdon, Oxfordshire OX14 4RN
52 Vanderbilt Avenue, New York, NY 10017

Routledge is an imprint of the Taylor & Francis Group, an informa business

First issued in paperback 2019

Library of Congress Cataloging in Publication Data
Names: Wolf, Mark J. P., author.
Title: The world of Mister Rogers' Neighborhood / Mark J.P. Wolf.
Description: New York: Routledge, Taylor & Francis Group, 2017. |
Includes bibliographical references.
Identifiers: LCCN 2017014963 | ISBN 9781138088115 (hardback)
Subjects: LCSH: Mister Rogers neighborhood (Television program)
Classification: LCC PN1992.77.M5773 W65 2017 | DDC 791.45/72–dc23
LC record available at https://lccn.loc.gov/2017014963

ISBN: 978-1-138-08811-5 (hbk)
ISBN: 978-0-367-88859-6 (pbk)

Typeset in Times New Roman
by Deanta Global Publishing Services, Chennai, India

Contents

Acknowledgments

I would like to thank Barry Keith Grant, Kristina Stonehill, and Annie Martin for initial encouragement; Brittany Smith at The Fred Rogers Company; reference librarian Christian Himsel; Ryan Pierson for pointing out video interview footage; Frenchy Lunning for an anecdote relating to the show; and Erica Wetter at Routledge and the anonymous reviewers for their enthusiasm for the book. Great thanks must go to Tim Lybarger and his website, *The Neighborhood Archive*, the best on-line sources for all things *Mister Rogers*; while many of the post-hiatus episodes can be watched or purchased on-line, very few of the pre-hiatus shows are available, and I am in great debt to the hundreds of hours of labor that it must have taken to post the information and screenshots from these episodes on-line (along with the post-hiatus episodes, as well). I also wish to thank Tim for reading and commenting on a draft of this book as well. Finally, I must thank the late Fred Rogers himself, for creating and communicating everything he did. I always held his show in high regard, and the research for this book has raised my estimation of it even more. Also thanks to my wife Diane, and my sons, Michael, Christian, and Francis, with whom I have watched and enjoyed so many episodes of *Mister Rogers' Neighborhood*. And, as always, thanks be to God.

Introduction

I went into television because I hated it so, and I thought there was some way of using this fabulous instrument to be of nurture to those who would watch and listen.

Fred Rogers[1]

In the realm of children's television, *Mister Rogers' Neighborhood* (1968–2001) was a unique program, and one which will never be duplicated. From the very start, Rogers had a new vision of what children's television could and should be, one which he developed and perfected over the years on the air. While the show may seem simplistic at first glance, repeated viewings of the program reveal an underlying complexity that one might not expect initially, including a carefully balanced and diverse set of characters and experiences, and the most elaborate imaginary world to appear in children's television, the ontology, geography, and rules of which extend beyond that of the mundane world. Though Fred Rogers' slow pace and clear manner of speech directed at young children have become the target of parody and are immediately evident on the show, a closer look reveals that, unlike many children's shows, Rogers' program neither condescended nor pandered to children, nor did he simplify things beyond what was necessary. He respected children and introduced them to a wide range of cultures and ideas (particularly in the area of music, Rogers' own specialty and one of his degree areas), in a style of presentation ranging from serious to surreal; the bizarre juxtapositions and weird situations occurring in some of the shows were on a par with anything *Twin Peaks* (1990–1) or *Medium* (2005–11) could dish up, but without being dark or gruesome, and the fact that they weren't makes them easier to overlook. The imaginary world of the program also grew and expanded over the years, and its level of complexity is also greater than what many viewers might suspect. Whimsical and wildly creative, Rogers nonetheless was always calm, composed, and attentive to his audience, and few television personalities have inspired parasocial relationships with their viewers in such numbers or intensity.

The show mixed location shooting with a variety of studio sets to build its world and welcomed guests like artists Andrew Wyeth, Peggy Lipschutz, Eric Carle, and Simon Rodia (who built the Watts Towers); musicians Yo-Yo Ma, Van Cliburn, André Watts, Itzhak Perlman, and Wynton Marsalis; entertainers Tony Bennett, Rita Moreno, Marcel Marceau, Margaret Hamilton, Bill Bixby, LeVar Burton, John Reardon, and the cast of *Stomp*; choreographer Tommy Tune; athletes Lou Ferrigno, Lynn Swann, and Olympic gold medalist Suzie McConnell; astronaut Al Worden; and more (actor Michael Keaton got his start on the show and worked as a production assistant). Through Picture Picture, Rogers included films of events like factory tours, which showed how various things are produced a step at a time with the industrial machinery involved, something that could even interest adults who had not seen such tours in person. And then, of course, there is the Neighborhood of Make-Believe, the heart of the program; Rogers was innovative in going beyond other shows, most of which merely used puppets on a stage who talked to humans (as in shows like *Kukla, Fran, and Ollie* (1947–57), *Howdy Doody* (1947–60), and *Captain Kangaroo* (1955–84); although *Howdy Doody*'s characters resided in Doodyville, the place was never developed to the degree that Rogers' Neighborhood of Make-Believe was). Rogers was also the host, writer, composer, and executive producer for his show. *Mister Rogers' Neighborhood* went on to outlast its competitors, and only *Sesame Street* (begun in 1969, a year after *Mister Rogers' Neighborhood*) has lasted as long. The continuing popularity of *Mister Rogers' Neighborhood*, even in syndication and on video, more than a decade after the production of the show's last episode, also demonstrates how it is deserving of milestone status.

The first chapter of this book, "Welcome to the Neighborhood", describes the structure and format of the show, examining its style and comparing it to other shows of its time, while the second chapter, "A History of *Mister Rogers' Neighborhood*", considers how the show developed out of Rogers' background and his earlier work on television, as well as how it changed and grew over the years, honing its effectiveness and uniqueness within the world of children's television. The third chapter, "The Neighborhoods: Interconnected Spaces and Places", examines the geography of the show's imaginary world and the way it structures and links its spaces with varying degrees of fantasy and reality, each of which is considered part of a neighborhood. Social structures of the world and the characters that people them are the topic of the next chapter, "The Neighbors: A Diverse Sociological and Ontological Spectrum", which details the broad range of characters that inhabit the neighborhoods of the show. Following that, the fifth chapter, "And I'll Have More Ideas for You: Ideology and the Neighborhood", looks at the ideas embodied in the show, the lessons and values it teaches children, and how they are taught to the television audience. Finally, the last chapter, "Mister Rogers' Legacy", examines the show's impact over time, its transmedia extensions, and the continuation of the company that made *Mister Rogers' Neighborhood*, Family Communications, which was later renamed The Fred Rogers Company. Following that is a list of some of the show's 895 episodes and their themes.

Although I grew up watching and enjoying *Mister Rogers' Neighborhood*, it was through watching it with my own children that I really came to appreciate the show, and my interest in imaginary worlds has caused me to consider it anew. Of course, none of the episodes that I saw as a child would be seen by my children; after producing 590 episodes over the years 1968 to 1975, the show went on hiatus for four years, returning in 1979 with 305 new episodes produced during the years 1979 to 2001. Since the show went into syndication in 2001, none of the pre-hiatus episodes are broadcast anymore. As of 2012, only a few stations showed *Mister Rogers' Neighborhood* five days a week, the way it was meant to be seen, while others show it once a week on Sundays. On-line, however, one can find twenty-six full episodes at http://pbskids.org/rogers/videos/index.html (as of early 2017), and other places like Hulu.com, Netflix, and Amazon.com.

Unlike many children's television shows, *Mister Rogers' Neighborhood* did more than simply entertain or occupy children's attention; it educated them in the affective domain, encouraging such things as appreciation for difference, collaboration, self-expression, and self-worth. The value of the affirmation of self-worth cannot be overestimated; not only did the show shape the future adults into which so many children would grow, Rogers's message directly affected, and can still affect, many adults as well. Dr. Frenchy Lunning, a faculty member at the Minnesota College of Art and Design, related the following story of what effect the show had on someone she knew:

> I have a friend who was from an immigrant family, with no money, and in order to put herself through college (she is very intelligent), she became a high-class call girl (she is also beautiful and a tremendous friendly vivacious personality). She told me that she got through the humiliation of that period by daily watching Mr. Rogers, so she could hear him say "And I like you just the way you are" every afternoon. She teared up just telling me this story. She is now a successful business manager of a well-known photographer in Chicago.

And Rogers's show did so much more than merely affirming children's self-worth; it also introduced them to the areas of culture, art, and music through guests, trips, art objects and processes, and demonstrations, making these accessible and meaningful in a way that a child could understand. At the same time, this also introduced them to an elaborate audiovisual imaginary world, the like of which they could not find elsewhere, even including non-Euclidean spaces (for example, building interiors like those of the Castle or Museum-Go-Round, which were far larger than their exteriors would suggest). While the educational content of children's television programming has improved greatly since the late 1960s, no other children's program has ever attempted such a fanciful mix of high art, low art, folk art, industrial production, learning in the affective and social domains, and more, all with a whimsical sense of humor, insight, and multiple levels of interconnected detail.

1   Welcome to the Neighborhood

Fred Rogers is a teacher. ... And what's so important about what Fred Rogers does on television is that it is unlike anything else on television. There is nothing else ... no one else like him. And what is he teaching? How to count to ten? No! How to name all the capitals in the United States? No! Here's what he's teaching: "You are like nobody else. There is only one person in the world like you, and ... people can like you exactly the way you are."

David McCullough, author and historian[2]

To understand both the uniqueness of *Mister Rogers' Neighborhood*, as well as its similarities with other children's television shows, one must first place the show in the context of its era and look at some of the other programs airing at the time, the "neighborhood" of children's television that Rogers' show would join. It was Rogers' attention to prosocial, affective, and experiential learning that led the way for other programs toward a more integrated and intentional approach—not by separating seriousness from play and fantasy from reality, but instead by integrating them carefully together in a way that children could understand while still challenging them to use their imaginations. While Rogers would not be the first to do many of the things he did, it was the way he combined them into the shape of a world, and the depth of detail and feeling that he gave them, that would finally lead to his hallmark style and his critical acclaim, popularity, and longevity.

Early Children's Television

Children's television had been around for over two decades when *Mister Rogers' Neighborhood* came on the air in 1968. The live nature of many shows meant a great deal of unscripted ad-libbing, as was the case on one of the most popular early shows, Burr Tillstrom's *Kukla, Fran, and Ollie* (1947–57), where Fran Allison was the human host who interacted with Tillstrom's puppets. Another show that relied heavily on puppet characters was *Howdy Doody* (1947–60), hosted by Buffalo Bob Smith. The show was performed in front of a live audience of children (the "peanut gallery") and involved both verbal and slapstick comedy; entertainment was the show's main goal, and there was relatively little educational content.

After playing the clown Clarabell on *Howdy Doody* and working on a number of other children's shows, Bob Keeshan hosted his own program, *Tinker's Workshop* (1954–8), and went on in 1955 to create the program for which he was best known, *Captain Kangaroo* (1955–84), which aired on CBS and later PBS. Keeshan did not talk down to his child audience, and unlike other children's shows of the time, *Captain Kangaroo*'s pace was gentle and calming, not exciting, a trait that would be shared by *Mister Rogers' Neighborhood* (Rogers was a guest on *Captain Kangaroo* in 1975, and Keeshan appeared in episodes 1126 and 1162 of Rogers' show). Like Rogers, Keeshan gave music an important role on the show, with "record productions", written to pre-existing pieces of music, and "operettas", including one based on Cinderella; the show's last program was a musical, "Lawrence the Lion". Although the show was based more on entertainment than education,[3] Keeshan was careful about what was shown, screening every commercial that would be aired on the program and rejecting exploitative advertising methods and certain kinds of toys (like war toys), sometimes to the chagrin of network executives, for whom this meant lost income.[4] At the same time, Keeshan was not above engaging in slapstick comedy, as his endurance of many showers of ping-pong balls on the program can attest (one can hardly imagine Rogers enduring such humiliation, even to entertain). Originally an hour-long program appearing five days a week, and performed live until the appearance of videotape recording technology, *Captain Kangaroo* had minimal time for planning and scripting; this kept the show from being able to contain coherent, multi-episode storylines or delve into issues the way *Mister Rogers' Neighborhood* would later be able to do.

The other long-running children's show with which *Mister Rogers' Neighborhood* is sometimes compared is *Sesame Street* (1969–present), which started a year after Rogers' show and also aired on PBS (Rogers appeared as a guest in episode 1575 of *Sesame Street* in 1981). Produced by the Children's Television Workshop, *Sesame Street* used a magazine format that had a rapid pace, with short segments that moved fast and changed often and were modeled after television commercials.[5] *Sesame Street* had a definite 1960s influence, according to Jane Henson, wife of Muppets creator Jim Henson:

> I guess I'm talking about the mid-sixties, mid-sixties on. You were just so enthused about everything ... and the idea of sitting children in rows in school—some of the confines of what had become established were just unacceptable; you just couldn't do it, and that's why I was, I don't know, but "Whoa, this isn't the way to learn!" ... That's one of the things that I love about *Sesame Street*, too, is that it holds on to some of that stuff that we knew from the sixties ... that life is a great explosion, that life is just a ball.[6]

Whereas *Mister Rogers' Neighborhood* concentrated on learning in the affective domain, valuing feelings and encouraging children's self-esteem and self-worth, *Sesame Street*, at its start, was mainly concerned with learning in the cognitive domain; things like letters, numbers, alike and different, and so on. According to *Sesame Street* creators Lloyd Morrisett, Joan Cooney, and Dr. Edward Palmer, *Sesame Street*'s main goal was to educate and entertain children who were at-risk in school, particularly the disadvantaged and those of a lower socioeconomic home background. As Executive Producer David Connell described it,

> In terms of setting, we decided to put it on an inner city street because that is something that an inner city child could identify with and we felt it might be helpful to them and it certainly wasn't going to be harmful to a kid from Larchmont.[7]

Not surprisingly, then, Lynette Kohn Friedrich and Aletha Huston Stein's 1973 study, *Aggressive and Prosocial Television Programs and the Natural Behavior of Preschool Children*, revealed that children from a higher socioeconomic standing tended to prefer *Mister Rogers' Neighborhood* more than those from a lower socioeconomic background.[8] While Rogers' program is not specifically targeted at any particular socioeconomic group, his neighborhood, world, and characters tend to be more middle-class and suburban, reflecting an environment similar to that of Rogers' own childhood in Latrobe, Pennsylvania.

Because of the specificity of their mission, *Sesame Street* was heavily dependent on and formed by research, making it the most heavily-researched television show in history.[9] Teaching was more direct on *Sesame Street*, and the setting and cast interaction conveyed a sense of the racial and gender equality that was to be part of the show's message. Lacking the funds and research staff that *Sesame Street* had, Rogers took a different approach, which combined his own background in ministry and music, leading more toward prosocial messages, affective learning, and arts appreciation (while *Sesame Street* also featured these things, they were not as central to the focus, at least initially). Rogers did employ research, too (discussed more in Chapter 2), but nowhere near the degree that *Sesame Street* did.

Interestingly, in its earlier days, *Sesame Street* tried shows with continuing plotlines reaching over the whole hour, but their research told them that children would lose the thread of the story.[10] Yet *Mister Rogers' Neighborhood* often had week-long storylines in the show's Neighborhood of Make-Believe segments that extended across five half-hour shows, which children were apparently able to follow easily; and sometimes it had continuing narratives across the television home segments at the same time.[11] Rogers' show even had more advanced intertextual references reaching across weeks, and even decades, of programming; see Chapter 3).

Sesame Street's emphasis on early education motivated *Captain Kangaroo* to move a bit more in that direction, and it certainly brought a faster pace to children's programming.[12] *Sesame Street*, however, due to its workshop funding, had a much larger budget to work with: about $28,000 per episode in 1969, compared with the $6,000 per episode cost of *Mister Rogers' Neighborhood* in 1968.[13] *Sesame Street* also had a greater ability to generate its own funding through licensing; by 1984, the Children's Television Workshop had made $200 million in character licensing, which helped to fund the show.[14]

But Rogers' goals did not need as much funding as *Sesame Street*; his show was only half an hour, and after 1979, he made far fewer episodes as well (averaging just under 15 a year, compared to *Sesame Street*'s 125 to 130 episodes per year), and the format of his program remained pretty much the same for the next twenty-two years, until he retired and the show ended in 2001. The regularity of the show's format was something children could rely on, and its familiarity could have a calming effect on its young audiences, yet there was enough variation to keep it interesting and fresh, for children as well as for the adult audience who watched the show with them, and for whom it was made.

A Typical Day in the *Neighborhood*

The show looks deceptively simple. Then you start looking at it, and realize how rich it is.

Hedda Sharapan, associate producer[15]

The format of *Mister Rogers' Neighborhood* is different than that of most children's shows, and Rogers himself described it as a "visit": "I don't think of our half-hours as 'shows' or even 'programs' as much as I consider them visits: television visits. I try to make them quiet and comfortable times with a caring neighborhood".[16] The neighborhood concept, then, is used throughout the show, which opens with a high-angle establishing shot of a neighborhood, the tabletop model neighborhood seen at the beginning and end of the show. The camera begins zoomed in on a building with an asymmetrical slanting roof: a building designed after the National Educational Television (NET) logo (the NET logo was actually incorporated into a building in the model, from November 10, 1969 to October 2, 1970, but then was replaced by a building with a similar shape; see Figure 1.1). As the music plays an instrumental piano rendition of the theme song, "Won't You Be My Neighbor?", the camera zooms out to show the neighborhood model (in later episodes, a track has been installed in the model and a miniature trolley is passing through), pans across it, and begins zooming back in on a little yellow house at the end of a road, the house representing the exterior of Rogers' television house. As the house is neared, we usually cut to the interior of the house, often to a close-up of the flashing yellow traffic light in between the front room and kitchen. Author Amy Hollingsworth suggests that the yellow light, meaning "caution", indicates that "it's time to slow down".[17] The camera then pans across the room to the front door, which opens as Rogers enters, singing the words to the song ("It's a beautiful day in this neighborhood"). This is not always the case, however; in episodes 1465, 1476, and 1483, for

Figure 1.1   The building with the asymmetrical roof in the neighborhood model over the years: in 1968 (episode 0094; top, left); in 1969 after the show's move to color (episode 1028; top, right); in 1979 (episode 1465; bottom, left); and in 1999 (episode 1746; bottom, right).

example, the camera tracks along the studio neighborhood exteriors outside the television house's front porch, Rogers walks into the shot, enters the house, and only then do we cut to the interior. In episode 1475, which introduces an opera, we track past the studio neighborhood exteriors and stop on Rogers' porch as he sits down on the swing, not even entering the house. Thus, most of the time in the opening sequence, even the blocking of the movement serves an educational purpose; Rogers walks in from left to right, and the Trolley enters the Neighborhood of Make-Believe from left to right, with both directions of movement deliberately designed to match the way children learn to read languages in the most of the Western world.[18]

In episodes in which Rogers enters the television house, this is the first point where variations typically occur; Rogers sometimes carries something as he enters the house, often obscured from view in a bag or box, which will become the object of discussion that the show will open with, after the song. As the song continues, so does Rogers' famous routine: the change from suit jacket to cardigan sweater (almost all Rogers' sweaters used on the show were knitted by his mother) and the change from dress shoes to sneakers, complete with a shoe tossed from one hand to another. Asked by a viewer why he tossed his shoe, Rogers replied,

> One day I was in an especially playful mood when our visit began, and I tossed my shoe. It was fun, and it's become a game between Mr. Costa, our musical director, and me. He tries to play certain notes on the piano just as I catch my shoe. Sometimes we do it together just right, and sometimes we don't, but it's fun for us to try each time because it's like a game.[19]

The shoe toss game is an example of the improvisational elements present on the show; unlike other shows, where music is prerecorded or added later in postproduction, the musical accompaniment and background music were performed live during shooting. This allowed the music to more closely reflect what was happening; for example, Rogers would talk about a certain subject, while Costa, adding quiet background music, would play an instrumental version of a Rogers song which related to the topic being discussed, a song that might have appeared in a past show, creating subtle intertextual musical references that only regular viewers could appreciate.

Once the sneakers are on, the show's topic is introduced in "conversation" with the "television neighbor". The object carried in may be used to introduce it, or Rogers may ask a question or use an anecdote to begin. From 1979 onward, the shows had weekly themes, beginning with the Monday episode. The themes were all topics to which young children could relate, and they are also used to identify the weeks of programming (see the list of episodes at the end of this book). Often, the theme would then lead into the introduction of a guest, or a visit to a guest, or a factory film on Picture Picture.

Frequently, Rogers leaves the television house to visit another location at this point, and we cut back to the neighborhood model, with the camera zooming out and pulling back from the little yellow house, panning across the scenery to the model of the new location, and then zooming in on it until the image cuts to the new location, either a real exterior in Pittsburgh that Rogers then enters or a studio interior of a fictitious location, like Negri's music shop or Brockett's

Figure 1.2 Comparisons between the neighborhood models and the actual
locations they represent: the model zoo entrance (top, left) and the
actual zoo entrance (top, right) from episode 1500; and the model
of Wagner's Quality Shoes (bottom, left) and the actual store
(bottom, right) from episode 1506.

bakery. Some of the real locations are even represented in the neighborhood model, allowing the program to cut from one to the other (see
Figure 1.2). This visit-within-a-visit then includes conversation with a
guest, usually with some kind of demonstration or performance, until
Rogers declares that it's time to go, smiling and beckoning his television neighbor to come along with him. Another shot of the neighborhood model returns us to the television house, where we cut back to its
interior as Rogers enters.

Other occasional items include "reveries" (as Newell calls them[20]),
which show someone's memories (like the McFeelys' wedding in episode 1476), imagined moments (as in episode 1025 when Rogers ima-
gines McFeely making a delivery in a kayak and we see it on-screen),
and other moments (like Rogers out walking the dog in a montage of
Pittsburgh neighborhood scenes in episode 1499). The most frequently

occurring feature, however, is Picture Picture, which shows short films (usually factory visits, showing the various stages of how something is made).

One of the filmmakers who made the films shown on Picture Picture was horror director George Romero (best known for *Night of the Living Dead* (1968) and its sequels), whose first paying job was working for *Mister Rogers' Neighborhood*. According to Romero's blog "Bloody Diary",

> My second job, one which actually did pay, was shooting a segment called "Picture, Picture" for Mr. Rogers' Neighborhood. Occasionally, after Fred had hung up his sweater and fed the fish, he would ask his trolley to bring a new episode of "Picture, Picture". A screen would open, the studio camera would push in, and a short film would be blue-screened.
>
> I shot a dozen or so of those short films. Some were meant to be educational (How Light Bulbs are Manufactured). Some were meant to be purely exploratory, to inspire thought in a four-year-old (Things With Wheels, Things That Feel Soft). Some were meant to defeat fears, to show that Mr. Rogers had to go through the same scary [*experience*] that a four-year-old had to go through sometimes, and that he came through it unscathed, so the four-year-old was likely to come through it unscathed, as well (Mr. Rogers Gets a Tonsillectomy).
>
> That was my first really big production. Mr. Rogers Gets a Tonsillectomy. It was shot in a real, working hospital. I had to quickly, and quietly, use my pin-lights (the ones from the hardware store) to get exposure in the waiting room, in Fred's bedroom, and in the O. R. I still joke that Mr. Rogers Gets a Tonsillectomy is the scariest film I've ever made.[21]

When the Picture Picture films ended, the camera would pull back from Picture Picture, returning the audience to Rogers' television house.

After a statement or two summing up the visit, film, or other event that just occurred, and perhaps a question for the viewer, Rogers indicates that it's time for some make-believe, and heads over to the window seat by the trolley track. There he either sets the stage for the Neighborhood of Make-Believe story (at the start of a five-episode series) or summarizes what has happened so far. The Trolley comes out, and we follow it with an iris-in as it departs down a tunnel in the back wall of the television house. Asked why a trolley was used, Rogers responded,

> There are a couple of reasons for that. First of all, we wanted to have a way of separating our Neighborhood (where things happen in a real way) from Make-Believe (where things can happen by pretending or by magic). Secondly, we wanted to show that we could all go together to another place—the Neighborhood of Make-Believe—by pretending. And thirdly, I suppose I decided to use a trolley on our program because when I was growing up here in Pennsylvania, there were lots of trolleys, and when I was a boy I liked taking rides on them.[22]

Next we cut and iris-out to another tunnel entrance as the Trolley emerges in the Neighborhood of Make-Believe. While this is the typical way the Neighborhood is entered, other means were also used; in the earlier shows, Rogers might look into a telescope and claim to see it, or the green flashing traffic light would be used to "go" there. Even on later episodes, Rogers might use a box decorated to look like the Trolley (as in episode 1620) or suggest we pretend a big soap bubble is the Trolley (as in episode 1507), and use them to make the transitions. In episode 1476, for instance, Rogers says, "Let's do something different, there are all kinds of ways to make-believe", and uses a zoom-in on some paper cups. No matter how the transition is made, a visit to the Neighborhood of Make-Believe almost always occurs within the program, though there are rare variations as well; in episode 1476 we have two separate visits, and in a few episodes there is no visit there at all due to a talent show (in 1281) and marionette performances (1350 and 1410) that take place instead.

The Neighborhood of Make-Believe narratives, at least in the post-hiatus shows, take place over a week's worth of episodes. While the portions of the show with Rogers talking to the viewer from his television house are the most directly educational, with books being read, objects being explained, and factory films and other demonstrations providing a variety of lessons and information, the sequences set in the Neighborhood of Make-Believe are designed as narratives, with their lessons more covertly embedded in cause-and-effect, trial-and-error interpersonal interactions between characters, in which viewers learn through vicarious experience. Both methods, which are used on most episodes, use different means to teach the same ideas, as both parts of the program are usually thematically related. As narrative, the Neighborhood of Make-Believe segments employ conflict in a way that is not found in the segments with Rogers in his television house and neighborhood; only rarely do we find misunderstandings and conflict there, whereas they are routinely present in the Neighborhood of Make-Believe.

The conflict driving the Neighborhood of Make-Believe narrative (when there is one) is usually the result of a misunderstanding, selfishness, a personality conflict, or characters' plans or schemes affecting others. These conflicts typically arise from the distinct and different personalities of the characters involved (see Chapter 4). Usually the conflict occurs between puppet characters; the human characters mediate between and help reconcile them, restoring peace, with a lesson in the affective domain occurring in the process. The use of puppets makes it easier to discuss issues that pertain to young children, and by giving them a narrative frame, a living example can be provided rather than merely an abstract discussion. Occasionally other devices, like mysteries, construction projects, or impending public events for which people are preparing (plays, fairs, operas, festivals, and so forth) are used to connect the five episodes of a week's programming, with the anticipated event happening in the fifth episode.

In most cases, the end of the Neighborhood visit is indicated by the Trolley returning into the same tunnel from which it emerged when the visit began. It then reappears in the television house, where Rogers comments on the action of the Neighborhood visit, drawing out a lesson from it or at least summarizing what happened. Next, there may be a continuation of an activity or use of props from before the visit or, less frequently, some interaction with a guest or neighbor. Most often, however, it is a time Rogers spends talking to the television viewer before wrapping up the show.

Rogers will also often feed the fish around this point in the program, but he does not do so on every program. While it may seem to be a small detail, younger viewers can be very concerned about the fish being fed. Rogers even received a letter from a blind five-year-old girl who asked him to say when he was feeding his fish because she couldn't see him do it; her father's note added that she cried if she thought they were not being fed.[23]

Rogers also cleans up props that he uses or, at the very least, indicates that he will clean them up later. Typically, he will return to the front room, where he begins changing back into his dress shoes and jacket, and segues into his closing song, which he sings while hanging his sweater back up in the closet; he leaves out the front door as the song lyrics ends (again, there are a few exceptions; for example, in episode 0018, he does none of these things). We cut back to the model as the camera zooms out from his house, pans across the neighborhood model, and finally zooms in, ending on the building with the asymmetrical slanting roof. The entire program, then, has a palindromic format that delves through levels of fantasy and then returns: from the streets of suburban Pittsburgh, as represented by the model, into Rogers' television house, into the Neighborhood of Make-Believe, and then back out again through the house and model (there are a few exceptions, however, like the operas, that take up an entire episode).

The relative regularity of the program's structure was designed to be a ritual, comforting and soothing to young audiences, who knew what to expect. Rogers' own life was likewise highly disciplined and regular; according to Hollingsworth,

> His daily routine was impeccably observed: he awoke at 5 a.m. for prayer, reflection, and Bible reading; took a 7:30 a.m. swim at the local pool (where he weighed in at exactly 143 pounds daily); followed his usual workday routine; and kept to a 9:30 p.m. bedtime.[24]

The regularity of the show's routine is also matched by the show's format, which remained virtually unchanged from 1979 to 2001. Even as times changed and the pace of television increased after the coming of MTV and a faster-paced life due to electronic technologies, Rogers' show kept to the same format, visual style, and performance style.

Visual Style and Performance Style

Mister Rogers' Neighborhood is perhaps most noted for its relaxed pace and lack of a flashy visual style. Other than a few transitional devices (like an iris in or out or focus in or out), the show rarely calls attention to formal aspects such as editing or lighting (an exception would be the operas, which are lit and shot more cinematically). All of this was to produce a slow, steady rhythm, calming and soothing, that young viewers could rely on, and that made Rogers' television visits more transparent (though he would occasionally reveal the technology behind the scenes and the fact that he was on a set, wanting to clearly distinguish fantasy from reality).

Although Rogers was a perfectionist who even scripted the ad-libbing of his guests to insure the quality of their remarks (a practice that made some guests, depending on their ability, seem less natural), the show's performance style included both real and simulated spontaneity. Often when Rogers would be talking to the viewer (or even singing), he would be interrupted by a phone ringing or a knock at the door, both of which he would answer with some degree of surprise (sometimes on his way over to the door he would even wonder aloud whom it might be). Likewise, sometimes guests or Mister McFeely would finish their visit by claiming that they "had to go", departing despite Rogers' invitation to stay longer. The formula could be reversed as well; in episode 1580, Chef Brockett asks Mister Rogers to stay for a treat with the children, and Rogers says he can't. In episode 1578, Rogers even has to go to a meeting, supposedly unexpectedly, leaving Chuck Aber to interact with his audience for a while in his absence. And in episode 1586, Rogers gets a phone call which turns out to be just a wrong number; as he doesn't say anything about the call afterward, it would seem it was included perhaps to make the show seem more spontaneous and unscripted, or to show how to react in such a situation. He also answers a wrong number call in episodes 1139 and 1595, and in episodes 1309 and 1468, he dials a wrong number himself and then apologizes; in the case of the latter two calls, there is, at least, the lesson of what to do if you misdial.

Some of the spontaneity was also real, as when mistakes were made and left in the program.[25] For example, in episode 1655, there's a knock at the door and Rogers says, "There's the doorbell", even though a doorbell is never used on the show. In episode 1692, Rogers drops his shoe during the shoe toss, and in episode 1077, Rogers ends up putting his sneakers on the wrong feet. In episode 0035, Rogers puts a small wooden stool on his head like a hat, thinks better of it, and removes it, saying, "I shouldn't do that. That might hurt a head". And in episode 1739, when Sylvia Earle brings an underwater microphone to listen to fish in an aquarium, she and Rogers are unable to get any sounds; yet the sequence was left as it was. In all these examples, these scenes could have easily been reshot, but the mistakes are left in, as a lesson that things do not always go as we hope they will. Episode 1576, the first program in the "Mister Rogers Talks About Making Mistakes" week of shows, begins with Rogers having difficulty getting his sweater zipped during the opening song. The mistake looks natural enough, until we realize that making mistakes is the theme of the show, suggesting that perhaps it was intentional. But then, after Rogers talks about it, he asks viewers if they remember the show when he buttoned his sweater wrong, and then shows the actual clip of a past show (episode 1293) where it did happen, actually foregrounding the fact that mistakes are made and left in the program (his zipper also snags his tie during the opening song in episode 1758, but the take is still used). Rogers must have also ad-libbed himself, at least in earlier programs; in episode 1013, for example, Betty Aberlin says a variety show will start in "201 seconds", to which Rogers responds, "That's a little over two minutes", even though it is exactly three minutes and twenty-one seconds.

Allowing mistakes to be included adds to the feeling of liveness and Rogers' own honesty (since he never considered himself an actor), and what writer Robert Bianco has called the "exaggerated ordinariness" of the show.[26] As Rogers said, regarding his role,

> I'm glad I can be a kind of father figure—not father surrogate ... Nothing electronic can ever take the place of a live human being to help them feel good about who they are. If people take what we do as a kind of hint as to what is possible in human relationships and just work toward it, great. ... I've never considered myself an actor. ... I've always just felt that I gave one more honest adult to the life of a child. And the more they can have, the better.[27]

As Hollingsworth points out, Rogers' attempt to be himself on the show also led to a certain degree of vulnerability, which itself carried a message for children:

> There were times when his vulnerability on the program made me almost embarrassed for him, like when he tried break dancing or the Charleston or was so wobbly on rollerskates that he almost fell.

Other times it was just amusing, like when he fumbled through a series of exercises, hopelessly mixing up the heads, shoulders, knees, and toes sequence and able to laugh at himself. But each example showed he was vulnerable; he was willing to try new things and keep trying new things even if he wasn't good at them. If Mister Rogers can be vulnerable, maybe even look foolish, well, then maybe it's okay for me too.[28]

The Neighborhood of Make-Believe segments, by contrast, are carefully scripted and acted, with far less of the simulated spontaneity and feeling of liveness found in the television house scenes. The scenery, like that of the television house, is perhaps more theatrical than cinematic in its realism, but the location is given more detail and complexity. Whereas other children's programs had stages for their puppet characters, which limited their appearances, the Neighborhood of Make-Believe is far more elaborate, with over a dozen locations where puppets can appear integrated into a neighborhood (see Chapter 3 for a detailed description of the neighborhood's geography). While clearly fantastic, the Neighborhood of Make-Believe is treated as a place with a history and is given a further degree of verisimilitude by appearing in varying conditions, including nighttime (as in episodes 0113, 1324, 1499, 1519, 1563, 1586–1590, 1702, and 1755), rainy weather (0120, 1510, 1571, and 1648), snowy weather (1514 and 1515), with skywriting in the sky (1643), a heat wave (1526 and 1527), and at sunset (1272 and 1701).

Finally, there are the show's operas, some of which take up an entire half-hour episode at the end of a five-episode continuity, and a play, *Josephine the Short-Neck Giraffe*, which spanned three episodes (1608–1610). Both human and puppet characters appear in elaborate costumes and sets, singing their lines, in fantastic and often surreal storylines. The acting style of the operas is, as one would expect, highly theatrical and dramatically exaggerated in contrast with the other episodes. Having neighborhood characters, including puppets, playing roles within an opera makes each a show-within-a-show, giving the show's viewers a dual-level performance (in which Neighborhood characters are sometimes even cast against type). The care given to the operas and to the Neighborhood of Make-Believe in general is also an example of the program's attitude toward play and seriousness.

Serious Play and Playful Seriousness

The notion of play is an important one on *Mister Rogers' Neighborhood*, and Rogers' multi-pronged approach included concepts we might call "serious play" and "playful seriousness", as opposed to a simple dichotomy of play and seriousness, both of which are parts of learning and growth. These topics and approaches arise in both the "real" neighborhoods and the make-believe ones, and certain issues, like the dignity, self-worth, and uniqueness of individuals, are always held sacrosanct regardless of the context in which they appear.

Much of the work of scholars Jerome and Dorothy Singer demonstrates the value of imaginative play in children's development. For example, they write,

> Pretending and the profound dimension of "as if" in human experience are intrinsic to the establishment of an efficient set of anticipatory guiding images, verbal labels, and plans with easily spun-out subroutines. Pretending itself depends on the level of the child's cognitive maturation and also the complexity or "realism" of the structures with which the child is dealing, as Fein (1975) had indicated in her experimental analysis of 18-month- to 2-year-olds simulating drinking from an empty cup or feeding a plastic "horsey" with invisible milk. ... there is increasing reason to believe that those children whose play repertory in the preschool period includes a good deal of make-believe and fantasy play have a distinct edge in certain important cognitive areas.[29]
>
> There is a body of evidence that suggests that by elementary school age children who show imaginativeness in spontaneous play or in projective test performance are less likely to be overtly aggressive or impulsive and are better able to tolerate delays or are more socially cooperative.[30]

While imagination is a subject encountered on many children's programs, few shows have as direct and overt discussions about it with children as Rogers' does, foregrounding the process and its uses and effects.

As mentioned earlier, the divide between the television house and the Neighborhood of Make-Believe also allowed the same theme to be presented twice, in different ways. Rogers in his television house can be seen as representing the "playful seriousness" side; he discusses issues directly with the viewer, gently and often playfully considering serious topics without rendering them inconsequential or suggesting they are irrelevant. His discussions also involve questions or "what if" scenarios for the viewer to consider, and occasionally there is inter-action or discussion with his visitors concerning the topic at hand. Rogers also continues the discussion when viewers return from the Neighborhood of Make-Believe segments.

On the other hand, in the Neighborhood of Make-Believe segments, the same issue will likely appear as part of the storyline and be dealt with more indirectly, by example, such as the various interpersonal conflicts that occur between characters (see Chapter 4). While some of the events and props may be outlandish, care is taken that emotional realism is maintained. Such "serious play" encompasses the develop-ment of a disciplined imagination and the methodical exploration of possibilities, while still remaining fantastic and whimsical. In episode 1471, for instance, King Friday even reminds Handyman Negri that they are just pretend; and in episode 1567, the schoolchildren (Daniel, Ana, and Tuesday) notice Chuck Aber operating H. J. Elephant, and then ask if they are toys as well. Together, these approaches are respon-sible for keeping the show both edifying and entertaining. The mixture of play and seriousness also requires the slower pace, allowing children to take things in and process them thoughtfully, and encouraging intel-lectual curiosity as well.

As Fred Rainsberry, former head of children's programming at the CBC in Canada, and the man who brought Rogers in front of the cam-era, explains,

> In the case of Mr. Rogers, there is no doubt about his conviction and the rightness of his approach. More importantly, he doesn't build his show upon the single proposition that slow pacing is better than fast pacing. His concern is for a one-to-one relation-ship with his young audience. ... I doubt that Fred Rogers has any exclusive concern that a child shall learn facts and make infer-ences. He is concerned with a child's sense of physical and social security and with helping the child to understand the nature of his physical and social environment, so that he will have the con-fidence to explore the world around him. He is concerned with that paradox of learning, being oneself while also accommodating oneself to the external world.[31]

Exploration, imagination, and the various ways play and seriousness can be combined are central to what the program teaches, rather than simply factual knowledge (like letters, numbers, and reading). The format for a television show that could be fun and entertaining while still educational in the affective domain came early in Rogers' career and provided the core around which the ideas for his show were developed and continued to be refined over the years.

2 A History of *Mister Rogers' Neighborhood*

With a television career spanning half a century, Fred McFeely Rogers became a television icon, yet he did not originally intend to appear on camera, and had grown up without television. Born in 1928, he was already nearing adulthood when the new medium became widespread, and though he professed to have watched very little television, what he did see made an impression on him and would help determine what his own show would be like. He had a message to deliver to the television audience, and his conviction, coupled with his background, training, and timing, resulted in the conditions necessary for his show to emerge.

Rogers' Early Career

In 1951, Rogers graduated with an undergraduate degree in music composition from Rollins College and planned to attend seminary after college. Seeing television, however, motivated him to alter the direction of his career: "I got into television because I saw people throwing pies at each other's faces, and that to me was such demeaning behavior. And if there's anything that bothers me, it's one person demeaning another. That really makes me mad!"[32] What he saw may have struck a chord because of his own background; as a shy, overweight eight-year-old boy, Rogers had been bullied by other boys, who taunted and chased him. Adults told him to shrug it off and pretend he didn't care, but even as a child Rogers knew this wasn't the right thing to tell a child, as though his feelings weren't legitimate.[33] From then on, he wanted to produce something for children that would let them know their feelings were as legitimate as those of others: that would be his message. Television would allow him to bring his message to a wide audience and, at the same time, use his musical skills as a composer. As Rogers stated,

> When I was a teenager, my expectation was that I would become a songwriter. Music was a big part of my life throughout my childhood and teenage years. I never expected to be on television. There wasn't such a thing as television when I was a boy. But I do compose the songs for our program, so in a way, I am fulfilling that expectation. I think what helped me was hard work and the grace of God.[34]

By the fall of 1951, Rogers was working for NBC in New York as floor manager for *NBC Opera Theatre* (1949–64), *Your Hit Parade* (1950–9), and *The Kate Smith Hour* (1950–4). Two years later, he came to Pittsburgh to produce *The Children's Corner* (1953–61) with Josie Carey; Rogers operated the show's puppets behind the scenes. Hedda Sharapan (director of special projects and associate producer of *Mister Rogers' Neighborhood*) describes the origin of the show as well as Daniel Striped Tiger's origins:

> In 1954 WQED was just getting off the ground. It was the first community-supported public station in the country. The others were all tied to universities. He (Rogers) was asked to come back here to be program director for this little station. His friends at NBC thought he was out of his mind to leave there for this tiny place. They (WQED) wanted a children's show and nobody was stepping up to do it, so he and Josie Carey, who was the secretary ... at the time paired up together and were to do this show. What was the show? It was just to be a bunch of films strung together, like nature films, things they got free from the library or schools. The night before the show was to go on the air there was a party given by Dorothy Daniel, who was head of WQED. She had set out a tiger puppet on the table, as just kind of this decoration, I understand.
>
> The next day they (Rogers and Carey) thought, "Well, we'll bring it in", and they had a sheet as a set, as the students had drawn things like a tree, a castle—I mean it was pure serendipity. They cut out the hole in the clock face. Fred Rogers put the tiger puppet on and Daniel (the tiger puppet) said something like, "It's 4:02

and Columbus discovered America in 1492". Daniel came off and Josie would introduce the films. What happened was the films would break because they were free things, old things, and as they broke what they had to do was fill and they filled with the puppets and Josie ... Then Fred said, "As we needed to fill more time we brought more puppets into it and this Neighborhood of Make-Believe was just a part of the whole set ... and it was an hour, live daily show".[35]

With a budget of $30 per episode, Rogers voiced and operated the puppets, composed the show's music, played the organ, and occasionally appeared on camera as a mysterious, masked prince who danced with Carey.[36] Besides Daniel Striped Tiger, other neighborhood puppets saw their debut on *The Children's Corner*, including King Friday XIII, Grandpere Tiger, Lady Elaine Fairchilde, X the Owl, and Henrietta Pussycat (who was a teacher of seventeen mice). Carey also had a toy train on the program that took viewers between the reality and fantasy sections of the show, making it a likely inspiration for the Neighborhood Trolley on Rogers' own show (that, and the fact that trolleys were used in Pittsburgh). The program also required the ability to improvise; as Kimmel and Collins write,

Much of the program was spontaneous, sometimes the result of a conversation at lunch. The humor and whimsy of the conversations were natural and spur-of-the-moment, but even in those early years Rogers was always conscious of the audience and their needs. If the humor was a bit of slapstick or seemed in any way to make light of children's feelings or emotions, Rogers would insist on discussing it later. Although Carey claimed that no one really "argued" with Fred, those "discussions" could be lengthy and involved.

The pair tried to involve the viewers as much as possible, and had a variety of guests from the community — representatives from the zoo, the symphony, a magician, or even someone to teach exercises. Since the program was live, there were problems everywhere at most anytime. One day someone called in sick and a University of Pittsburgh student who was walking by the station was asked to help. When he asked what he was to do, the casual answer was, *oh, you know, just operate the camera.*[37]

The pace and demands of *The Children's Corner* meant finding enough material to fill an hour a day, leaving little time for educational concerns. As Rogers told interviewer Lucille Burbank,

> with *The Children's Corner*, we just wanted to have a presence between five and six every afternoon. There wasn't something for children in Pittsburgh in those days. ... And I don't think we had any kind of lofty notion about what the philosophy of this program would be. We were all so busy. ... These were the exciting, early days of a medium. ... I wish I could give you a highly philosophical answer.[38]

While working in television, Rogers attended the University of Pittsburgh's Graduate School of Child Development, as well as Pittsburgh Theological Seminary, where he enrolled in lunch-time classes which he attended for eight years, finally finishing in 1962. It was there, in a counseling class, that he met Dr. Margaret B. McFarland, director of the Arsenal Family and Children's Center, who would become his chief consultant and advisor. He was ordained a Presbyterian minister, and was called to serve children and families through mass media. His ordination gave him a different outlook regarding the purpose of children's television, which would be reflected in the programs he was to host.

From *Misterogers* to *Mister Rogers' Neighborhood*

> *In 1962, when I graduated from Pittsburgh Theological Seminary, I joined the Canadian Broadcasting Corporation in Toronto, where Dr. Frederick B. Rainsberry (head of CBC children's programs) told me, "Fred, I've seen you talk with children. I want you to translate that to television." I doubt if I would ever have "faced" a camera if it hadn't been for his encouragement. ... (It was also Fred Rainsberry's idea that the program should be called* Misterogers. *When I returned to Pittsburgh, we called the program* Misterogers' Neighborhood *and then later changed it to* Mister Rogers' Neighborhood, *out of a concern for viewers who were learning to read.)*

Fred Rogers[39]

Fred Rainsberry of the CBC invited Fred to come to Canada to do a 15-minute children's program there and suggested Rogers be in front of the camera rather than behind it. And so the program *Misterogers* (1963–6) began. According to Sam Newbury, supervising producer of *Mister Rogers' Neighborhood,*

> Josie was a very high energy person, but Fred loves to improvise and fool around, in fact very quick witted, but I think—he went to Canada after about eight or nine years of this and Fred Rainsberry convinced Fred to go on camera and Fred's on-camera presence, like his real presence, tends to be a fairly deliberate, you know, calm type of presence. So, that when he became the on-camera person it really changed the structure and rhythm of the show, and his love of puppets—the puppets were always part of a show, and under the influence of Dr. Margaret McFarland, his main consultant, the puppet segment and the segment with Fred on camera became more clearly defined and more clearly separated. There used to be a sort of flowing back and forth … I think Dr. McFarland worked on the question of helping kids understand fantasy, what was fantasy and how to use it, and the clearer the demarcations the more useful it was.[40]

After three years, Rogers and his wife found their visas expiring and decided to move back to the United States. Rogers acquired the rights to his show in 1966 and moved it to WQED in Pittsburgh, renaming it *Misterogers' Neighborhood.* The Eastern Educational Network bought 100 episodes, which were broadcast regionally, and the show was cancelled in 1967 due to lack of funding. But public outcry at the cancellation resulted in new funding from the Sears Roebuck Foundation, and the show moved to nationwide broadcasting on National Education Television (NET).

The new show began airing February 19, 1968, and later appeared on PBS when it replaced NET. During the first season, 130 shows were produced, all in black and white, with budgets around $6,000 to $10,000 per episode.[41] After that, 65 episodes a year, all in color, would be produced, up to and including the eighth season in 1975. Concerned about children learning to spell, Rogers also changed the program's name to *Mister Rogers' Neighborhood,* separating the words, beginning with the first show of the fourth season in 1971. David Newell (who played Mr. McFeely, a.k.a. "Speedy Delivery") described the early days of the show:

> Let's take a typical day twenty years ago [1970]. We would get our scripts that Fred would have written during the summer. Let's say in September we would start again, which we did. Fred would spend all summer writing scripts, as many as he could get done. ... He would have some rough outlines or outlines of the scripts and some scripts written when he came back ... I would get the scripts and at that point I would be the one who was in charge of getting all the props for anything we needed, so I would identify all of the props I needed, starting my search for whatever.
>
> Fred (Rogers) concurrently would be consulting with Margaret (McFarland) and going home that evening and writing even more programs ... Diana, who was doing our films at that point, would identify how many films she needed to do, to insert into the program and research those—how light bulbs are made ... how a dishwasher works, etc. Hedda Sharapan [*writer, director of special projects, and associate producer*], at the same time, would be getting calls in to some of the talent, arranging some of the people to come in who are the regulars, giving them scripts, and our director would be arranging studio time, talking to the designer about what sets we may need, etc. All of this would be going on— then preparing for the first day in the studio.[42]

Having over a decade of experience in children's television, and several years of doing his show in Canada, Rogers had a grasp on his mission and had adjusted his format to fit it. Describing his on-screen role in a 1992 interview, Rogers stated,

> We really wanted to give children a visit from an uncle-like person, a neighbor who—I think that almost anybody who has had parents who work most of the day and they turned out to be interested, interesting people have said, "You know there was always a neighbor; there was a librarian; there was a teacher; there was somebody who really seemed to care about me". You can hear that from kids who have grown-up into the professions, often.[43]

In 1975, Rogers decided to take a break and put the show on hiatus to work on other projects, including a PBS television show for adults,

Old Friends ... New Friends (1979–81), a show about intergenerational relationships, which he hosted and executive produced. As a result, in 1976, only five new episodes of *Mister Rogers' Neighborhood* aired, one week's worth during February 16–20. During these episodes (1456–1460), Rogers prepares his young viewers for reruns, actually showing a shelf containing dozens of videotapes of Neighborhood visits and telling his audience, "Next week we'll start to show all of these visits so everybody can see them the whole way through" (episode 1456). The entire week of shows features Rogers and others looking back on older episodes and watching scenes from them. Meanwhile, in the Neighborhood of Make-Believe segments of these episodes, Margaret Hamilton returns as Margaret Witch with her crystal ball showing future scenes of the Neighborhood residents, as if to reassure viewers that the Neighborhood had a future. After two seasons of producing *Old Friends ... New Friends*, Rogers returned to working on the *Neighborhood*, with the first new episode in over three years appearing on August 20, 1979.

The Post-Hiatus Years

During the remaining years of the show, 1979–2001, there were 305 episodes produced, with week-long storylines and themes spanning five episodes designed to air Monday through Friday. Since the show continued solely through reruns during the hiatus, it could continue to do so to some extent, so fewer new episodes were needed; and as one group of children grew up and no longer watched the show, a younger group took its place who had never seen the earlier shows. Five episodes were produced in 1979, 10 in 1980, 15 in 1981, and 20 in 1982; and from 1983 onward, 15 episodes were made every year, except for 1993, 1994, 1997, and 2000, which each had 10 episodes, and 2001, the show's final year, when only 5 episodes were made. With week-long themes and continuities, the shows were more structured and planned, more factory films and remote locations were used, and the pace of these shows was a little faster than that of the earlier ones. Talking about the newer shows, producer Sam Newbury commented,

> There's less time, I think, spent very quietly with Fred by himself talking to the child at home. There used to be more sort of making—you know, Mister Rogers would sit down in the kitchen and make something. I remember when I first came I watched an

old show, one of the very early shows in which he was painting the porch swing [*episode 1007*] and I watched it and as it started I sort of said, "Okay, now where is going to be the cut away where we see Fred smile and we come back and the swing is going to be mostly painted?" How are they going to cut through this and condense the time? And then as it went on I realized they were not going to and Fred was going to paint the whole bench (swing) in real time in the program, and he did. I don't think we do that any-more ... I think probably our pacing has quickened somewhat just out of societal influence. Nothing is as slow as it was before. ... I do think the pacing is integral to the show and in fact if the show became a fast-paced show not only would it be something dif-ferent, but it probably wouldn't work. It's really based on a very deliberate communication with time to react and time to think, time to absorb.[44]

But the pace of the show was still slower than most television, and Rogers received many letters from parents who were thankful for the show's relatively slow pace.[45] A number of studies have revealed the value of a slow pace, including the oft-cited 1973 study by Friedrich and Stein mentioned earlier, and those by Jerome Singer and Dorothy Singer, who write in *Television, Imagination, and Aggression: A Study of Preschoolers*:

The study by Friedlander, Wetstone, and Scott (1974) suggest that children prefer much more slowly paced sequences of informa-tion presentation and can comprehend a good deal of material if not burdened with too hectic a pace. Our studies of recall mate-rial from "Mister Rogers' Neighborhood", a slow-moving child-oriented program, suggests that the less-intelligent child can recall more because of Mister Rogers' soft speech and careful repeti-tion (Tower, Singer, Singer, & Biggs, 1979). We also noticed that although children's eyes wander from the set during that show and the youngsters even go off to play they can retain as much or more of what they have seen as children who stayed glued to "Sesame Street".[46]

Though Rogers' show always had educational aspects, the post-hiatus shows presented their educational content more overtly, concentrating on a particular theme for each of its week-long continuities, such as Competition, Discipline, Making Mistakes, Going to School, Day and Night Care, and even Divorce (see the list of episodes at the end of this book). Rogers would have weekly meetings with Dr. McFarland, and topics grew out of their conversations, as well as viewer's requests, staff meetings, or other things Rogers thought were important. David Newell called Rogers an "interpreter", saying, "he'll take a very complex issue such as divorce and try … to interpret that for a preschool child in a very supportive and nonthreatening way, and I think that in some ways is the purpose of the program, to take the world and synthesize it for a very young child".[47] Rogers had more time for planning and production, averaging slightly less than three weeks of programs a year for the remainder of the show's run (1979–2001). Though the show looked largely improvised and effortless, it was not as simple as it looked. As Kimmel and Collins write,

> As Rogers recalled, there was a sequence to producing the program. The field trips or remote sites such as factory videos were usually completed first, but some remotes took longer than others. The Neighborhood of Make-Believe episodes were worked through before the interiors in his television house were shot. He estimated that for every minute on the air, there was at least an hour of production. Rogers said, "That doesn't count the script writing, telephone calls and production meetings. It may look effortless and so it should. But much time and effort goes into just one half-hour program". All those concerned with the program insist that the content was primarily Rogers', although often cast and crew were included in the development of a particular theme or issue. Regular contact with McFarland, who encouraged Rogers' creativity, was also a part of the program's growth. Some scenes were repeated seven or eight times until Rogers was satisfied. One of the staff might say that this part needed to be a bit faster or that something would look better in a different place, but the script—the content—was Rogers' alone. … Despite these rare instances when mistakes were deliberately kept in, each segment was very carefully planned—a real difference from the far more impulsive Children's Corner. Yet the program retained the look of an in-the-moment program, helping to keep the young audience interested. One web blogger recently commented, "I don't

think Mister Rogers' Neighborhood is scripted per se except in the Make-Believe segment. I think there's an ad lib element that's key to the show's charm"—showing that even adults can be fooled by the seamless, spontaneous nature of the program.[48]

Just as the feeling of liveness made the show seem spontaneous, the simplicity of its themes and messages may give the impression that the show itself was simple; but as I show in the chapters ahead, there is much going on that is easy to miss with only intermittent or casual viewing.

When Rogers retired in 2001, several generations of children had grown up with the show and now recognized him as a television icon, whose long, on-going presence on PBS placed him among the likes of Lawrence Welk, Julia Child, and Louis Rukeyser. Like these figures, Rogers had millions of audience members who had established a parasocial relationship with him, many from a very early age. The idea of parasocial relationships was suggested in a 1956 essay by Donald Horton and R. Richard Wohl, who almost sound as if they are describing Rogers' show when they write,

The persona offers, above all, a continuing relationship. His appearance is a regular and dependable event, to be counted on, planned for, and integrated into the routines of daily life. His devotees "live with him" and share the small episodes of his public life—and to some extent even of his private life away from the show. Indeed, their continued association with him acquires a history, and the accumulation of shared past experiences gives additional meaning to the present performance.[49]

Indeed, one critic, *New York Observer* writer Aaron Gell, has even suggested that the intensity of Rogers' parasocial relationship with the viewer "encouraged a deeply personal relationship to television that did more harm than good".[50] Well aware of his effect on his fans, Rogers always encouraged people to think of others who were close to them, something he even encouraged during his acceptance speech for his Lifetime Achievement Award Emmy in 1997, when he called for ten seconds of silence for the audience to think of those who helped them.

Human relationships, how one feels about oneself and others, and the management of relationships with other people are at the heart of

Mister Rogers' Neighborhood. "Neighborhood" implies a place and spatial structure as well as a set of neighbors, the beings who inhabit the neighborhood ("neighborhood" could also refer to the condition of being a neighbor, similar to the words "manhood" or "childhood"). Thus, we can examine the show from the point of view of geography (see Chapter 3) as well as ontology (see Chapter 4).

3 The Neighborhoods

Interconnected Spaces and Places

Fictional geographical settings for children's shows appeared as early as Doodyville on *Howdy Doody* (1947–60), the "Treasure House" of *Captain Kangaroo* (1955–84), and, of course, the eponymous street of *Sesame Street* (1969–present). Of these, the latter comes closest in size and complexity to the world of *Mister Rogers' Neighborhood*, with over a dozen locations (including exteriors and interiors) and a decades-long history. Though more realistic and less fanciful than the Neighborhood of Make-Believe, Sesame Street is still an idealized place, cleaner and less vandalized than its real-life counterparts in urban New York City. But the variety of interconnected settings, each occupying a different position along an ontological spectrum bridging and mixing fantasy and reality, along with conventions that limited the travel between them, gave the imaginary world of Rogers' program an existence different from that of any other show on television.

Mister Rogers' Neighborhood could have just as easily been named in the plural form, as there are several different neighborhoods comprising the geography of the show. There are the actual streets of suburban Pittsburgh that Rogers can be seen walking along on his way to various real locations; the television neighborhood of "realistic" studio sets, including the interior and exterior of Roger's television house as well as the studio-set interiors of other buildings like Joe Negri's music shop, Don Brockett's bakery, François Clemmons's music studio, Betty Aberlin's theater, Elsie Neal's craft shop, Robert Trow's workshop, Tony Chirolde's Costume, Book, and Toy Shop, and Mr. McFeely's home; the miniature tabletop model of suburban Pittsburgh seen at the beginning and end of each show; the Neighborhood of Make-Believe and adjacent areas; and the tabletop model of the Neighborhood of

Make-Believe that Rogers stores on his kitchen shelf (and the drawing of it that hangs on the kitchen wall). Finally, there are the non-neighborhood spaces, the factory interiors seen in the films and the non-diegetic studio spaces occasionally revealed on the show. Most of these spaces are joined together by the Neighborhood Trolley, which passes through them, acting as a unifying element, and which also became an icon representing the show itself. Rogers' masterful use of interconnected spaces, and his effortless navigation of them, is not only an element of the show's success and uniqueness, but also his way of connecting and combining the gaps between fantasy and reality, play and seriousness, and even childhood and adulthood.

The "Real" Neighborhoods: Pittsburgh and the Television Neighborhood

Many of the remote locations appearing on the show, as well as many of the show's guests, were from the Pittsburgh area. During the transitions to these various locations, we see scenes of the actual streets of Pittsburgh, intercut with the neighborhood model representing them. By combining models of actual places (like Wagner's shoe store) along with models of fictitious places (like Rogers' television house), Rogers wove his television neighborhood into the streets of suburban Pittsburgh (see Figure 1.2). Thus, instead of having a sharp divide between fantasy and reality, as many authors or commentators have suggested, there are instead differing degrees and mixtures of fantasy and reality represented by different sets of spaces on the program. Other actual places are also seen in the factory films shown on Picture Picture, some of which are filmed outside of Pittsburgh as well. Occasionally, Rogers would go to places outside of Pittsburgh and show footage of the trips, including the Butler County Mushroom Farm in Winfield, Pennsylvania (in episode 1489), the Edible Schoolyard in Berkeley, California (in episode 1751), or the ocean in which he went snorkeling with Sylvia Earle (in episode 1619).

While some of the locations have real exteriors and interiors, like Betty Aberlin's house, the Wagner shoe store, and the restaurant where Audrey Roth works, other location interiors, treated much in the same way, are studio sets. Brockett's bakery, Negri's music shop, and Robert Trow's workshop all have representative buildings in the neighborhood model, but no life-size exteriors to show, so unlike the actual locations, which typically cut from the model, to the exterior, to the interior, the model cuts directly to the interior of the television neighborhood locations. The only exceptions are the McFeely house, which is not seen very often, and Rogers' own television house, which has an exterior complete with front porch and yard, beyond which a few building exteriors extend for wider shots. Although Rogers does occasionally talk about how his television house is not a real house or the one he lives in (in episode 1497, for example, he calls his wife at his real home (or at least appears to)), many younger viewers assumed that it was his real house.[51]

The television house is made up of several areas; moving from left to right, there is the front yard, the porch, the front room, the kitchen, and a backyard area, reached by a back door in the kitchen. Another space, the bathroom, is shown far less (for example, in episodes 1012, 1614, 1665, 1686, 1699, 1723, 1741, and 1742). The bathroom is supposedly adjacent to the kitchen, but there is no door seen in the kitchen that could lead to it. To get to the bathroom, Rogers walks off-screen (perhaps implying the door exists in the "fourth wall" through which we view the interior) and the scene cuts to the bathroom. This absence of a concrete connection suggests that the addition of a bathroom may have been an afterthought, perhaps due to viewers' questions; Rogers received at least one letter in which a child did not believe that Rogers ever defecated, because he did not see any bathroom in the house.[52] Also, since the bathroom has a working sink, toilet, and bathtub (as Rogers demonstrates), it appears to be an actual bathroom and not simply a studio set, which is intercut with the studio rooms. Shown even less is the television house's garage/workshop, which we see in episodes 1456–1460. To get there, Rogers walks to the right through his backyard, past the sand table, and behind a wooden building on the right. We cut to him walking as seen from a window inside the garage (a smoother transition than merely walking off-screen), and then he enters through a door in the back. The garage location takes advantage of ambiguity in the Neighborhood model; while the sand table in the backyard is sometimes visible in the model, it is unclear if the detached garage is there, as it is obscured by a gray building. Finally, the least-seen room of the television house is the "little room over by the bathroom" where Rogers keeps a computer and does his writing (see Figure 3.1). This room was the last to be added and is shown in episode 1746, which also introduces viewers to the "on-line

Figure 3.1 The "little room over by the bathroom" is seen in episode 1746. This room was a late addition to the television house and was used to introduce a computer into the program in 1999.

neighborhood", the *Mister Rogers' Neighborhood* website, which adds a virtual space to all the other ones.

Adding to these spaces, Rogers demystifies the process of making a television program by breaking the fourth wall and crossing it in episodes 1486, 1530, and 1546. In 1546, for example, the camera follows him as he walks out of the television house, past the edge of the set, and across the studio floor (see Figure 3.2). In the background, we can see the lit set-up of the neighborhood model, connecting it to the studio space. Rogers continues walking, goes over to the musicians (who produce the show's live musical accompaniment), and introduces them to the television viewer, thus connecting the diegetic and nondiegetic spaces of the program. In episodes 1531 and 1681, he demystifies the Trolley, showing and demonstrating its controls; and in episode 1457, he shows the inner workings of Picture Picture. Going even farther, in episode 1698 Rogers shows a time-lapse film of the entire television house being built on the sound stage.

Figure 3.2 Rogers breaks the fourth wall and shows the audience the studio in a high-angle shot in episode 1530 (top, left and right), and in eye-level shots in episode 1546 (center, left and right). In episode 1468, he shows viewers the neighborhood model (bottom, left and right).

The house has several links to the Neighborhood of Make-Believe; in the kitchen, there is a drawing of it on the back wall, and on the shelf are miniature models of its various locations (the models were built by Robert Trow and given to Rogers during the early years of the show). Sometimes the model is used for the transition to the Neighborhood of Make-Believe, but the most often used connection is in the front room:

the trolley track and tunnel that leads into the wall, and leads into the iris-in/iris-out that marks the transition from one realm to the other.[53]

Thus, even without the Neighborhood of Make-Believe, there are already multiple ontological levels present.

The Neighborhood of Make-Believe and Surrounding Areas

Originally, there was an even looser division between the television neighborhood and the Neighborhood of Make-Believe. In the early episodes, more crossover occurs between the two places, and the people of the Neighborhood of Make-Believe seem more aware of what is going on outside of it. Rogers is able to see the Neighborhood of Make-Believe from his living room through a telescope, as though it were geographically connected; Daniel sends a note to Rogers; and Rogers receives phone calls from puppet characters. While visiting his television house, Betty Aberlin talks with Rogers about the Neighborhood of Make-Believe, and Rogers gives things to guests who are passing through and on their way there. In later shows, Rogers is the only one to acknowledge the existence of the Neighborhood of Make-Believe, and its residents no longer seem to have contact with, or knowledge of, the outside world, making the division of fantasy and reality more distinct. In the post-hiatus episodes, human cast members (like Betty Aberlin and Robert Trow) are themselves in Rogers' neighborhood, and slightly renamed characters (like Lady Aberlin and Robert Troll) in the Neighborhood of Make-Believe. Only Mr. and Mrs. McFeely still pass freely between the two realms and remain their fictional selves.

Like the television house, the Neighborhood of Make-Believe is laid out (and often experienced, due to the trolley) from left to right. On the far left is the Eiffel Tower (reflecting Rogers' minor in French while at Rollins College), then the trolley track and Castle, Corney's[54] Factory, the Oak Tree where Henrietta and X the Owl live, the Museum-Go-Round, the Platypus Mound (originally a frog pond in the earliest episodes), and Daniel's Clock. Another space exists behind the back wall, between the factory and the Museum-Go-Round; in episodes 1508 and 1510 we find out there is a garden back there, a large area with a colored path, white bridge, picnic area, and what appear to be mountains in the distance (in one of the few views looking in the direction of the fourth wall, from which the show is normally seen, a kind of distant mountain can be seen in episode 1508). Most of the locations also have interiors, built as separate sets, in which scenes occur when characters (including the human characters) go inside them. The Castle and the Museum-Go-Round have numerous rooms which are referred to, some of which are shown, and they have the most spacious interiors. The factory, Platypus Mound, Henrietta Pussycat's house, and X the Owl's home in the Oak Tree all have interiors as well, albeit smaller ones. All of the interiors, however, are much larger than their exteriors imply, making their spaces appear to be non-Euclidean ones, and probably the first examples of non-Euclidean space that children will have encountered.[55] The motive for the differences in size is, of course, a practical one, yet the end result is still something that stimulates and encourages a child's imagination.

The Neighborhood of Make-Believe is the center of activity in the Make-Believe segments, but there are other areas surrounding it as well; in episode 1618, Lady Aberlin shows Handyman Negri a map with all of the places laid out in it, which also shows them linked by trolley tracks. These places were added over time as the lands of Make-Believe expanded. In first few weeks of the program in 1968, a new character, Donkey Hodie, appears in the Neighborhood, looking for a place to build his windmill. King Friday allows him to build it behind the Castle, but later changes his mind and tells him it must be built someplace else. Donkey Hodie searches for another place, and ends up building his windmill at Someplace Else, an area to the east of the Neighborhood of Make-Believe (further extending the left-to-right layout mentioned earlier). Later, Harriet Elizabeth Cow builds a schoolhouse in Someplace Else (see Figure 3.3), and Hodie's windmill can be seen outside the schoolhouse's window.

The other areas are named for their locations relative to the main Neighborhood: Westwood, home of Mayor Maggie and Neighbor Aber (and former home of Sara Saturday, before she married King Friday and became Queen); Southwood, home of Betty Okonak Templeton Jones and her husband James; and Northwood, home of Old Goat and referred to by King Friday as "a predominantly goat neighborhood" in episode 1620. Scenes and celebrations, like the Bass Violin Festival in Southwood (episode 1550), take place in these areas, and they also provide material for the central conflicts of some of the storylines (like the overflowing dumps during the Environment week episodes (1616–1620), or episode 1522, when King Friday has the neighbors come

Figure 3.3 Stages of the building of the schoolhouse in Someplace Else: the foundation is laid in episode 1462 (top, left), the framing is completed in episode 1464 (top, right), and in episode 1465, the exterior is completed (bottom, left) and the interior is ready (bottom, right).

to the Castle to assemble bombs, mistakenly fearing that Southwood is preparing bombs to attack his kingdom). Just as the Neighborhood of Make-Believe residents demonstrate conflict and resolution on a neighborly scale, the surrounding areas act collectively as Neighbors at the community scale, showing how communities work together, internally and with each other, in order to solve problems.

Beyond the four cardinal directions, there are also places located above and below the Neighborhood of Make-Believe. Above, beyond the sky, is Planet Purple, the discovery of which is announced by Lady Elaine in episode 1237, and which is seen through a telescope in episode 1563; it is the home of the alien Purple Panda, who visits the Neighborhood from time to time. Below the Neighborhood is an old underground tunnel between the Oak Tree and the Platypus Mound, which the neighbors discover in episodes 1678–1679 and explore in episode 1680; characters also go underground while digging a hole for a pool in episode 1528; and in episode 1530, new water pipes are being installed underground, and scenes are shown of the new tunnel as characters don miner helmets and go down inside to have a look.

Finally, a few places, seen more rarely or only mentioned, are less integrated into the other spaces. In episode 1476, the Royal Family is out having a picnic at a "picnic place", which seems to be wilderness with what appear to be small mountains in the distance; the place is not given a distinct geographic location relative to the Neighborhood. Also, there is the Land of Allmine, from the earlier years of the show, and Shadyville, mentioned in episode 1676 as the home of Cousin Mary Owl.

Neighborhood characters also appear in each theatrical diegesis-within-a-diegesis used for the operas; some of the most fantastic, surreal, and elaborate sets appear in the operas, though where the operas themselves are supposedly being staged within the Neighborhood of Make-Believe (or even if they are) is not always indicated. These include such whimsical places as Bubbleland, Spoon Mountain, Otherland, and Balindore, the last of which is entered through a door in a doorframe standing alone on a mountainside; Balindore has a spacious lodge-like interior, but no exterior other than just the doorframe (this is the only time that attention is called to the non-Euclidean nature of such a space).

Just as Rogers demystifies the studio space for his young viewers, he also goes behind the scenes and shows how the Neighborhood of Make-Believe operates in episode 1384, which aired in 1974. On this episode, Rogers demonstrates how the puppets work and shows a behind-the-scenes film showing the backsides of the sets and the puppeteers. In calling attention to the workings of the show, Rogers helps his young audience become more sophisticated television viewers, and media viewers in general, able to enjoy the illusion of an imaginary world while at the same time having an understanding of how that world is created. And, as mentioned earlier, the imaginary world Rogers created was one of the most detailed and elaborate ones found in children's television.

World-building and Intertextual References

The Neighborhood of Make-Believe and the regions surrounding it were built up and developed over the years the program aired. The Neighborhood itself began forming on *The Children's Corner* (where

King Friday was originally King of Calendarland) and continued in Rogers' Canadian show; in the first few weeks of *Mister Rogers' Neighborhood*, the new area of Someplace Else was added. Eventually Westwood, Southwood, Northwood, and other areas would fill in the map, as described above. Existing areas would also see further development over time; the Frogg Pond was replaced with the Platypus Mound when the Frogg family moved to Westwood and the Platypus family moved to the Neighborhood early in the second season of the show, and in episodes 1461–1465, Harriet Elizabeth Cow's schoolhouse was planned and built in Someplace Else, with the building being seen at various stages of its construction (see Figure 3.3).

Besides the continuing and overlapping stories of pre-hiatus episodes and the week-long narratives connecting post-hiatus episodes, there are other events which add to the overall story of the Neighborhood, giving it a history. The appearance of new characters and their presence in subsequent episodes, like the birth of Ana Platypus in episode 1104 or Prince Tuesday in episode 1117, give the viewing audience and the show's characters a set of events that can be referred to in later episodes, rewarding long-time viewers. The Neighborhood's historical timeline is further developed through the inclusion of scenes set in the past and future; for example, in episode 1668, the Trolley shows an image of what the Neighborhood of Make-Believe looked like back when it was mostly open land, with places appearing in the order they were built (Daniel's Clock, the Castle, the Oak Tree, the Museum-Go-Round, the Eiffel Tower, the Factory, and the Platypus Mound). In episode 1454, actress Margaret Hamilton appeared on the show, and in the Neighborhood of Make-Believe as "Margaret Witch", whose crystal ball could show scenes of the past and future. In her crystal ball, we see a past scene of pianist Van Cliburn playing the piano upside-down at the wedding of King Friday and Queen Sara, as well as a vision of the future in which Prince Tuesday and Ana Platypus are adults (along with new puppets to represent their adult forms). In episode 1670, King Friday asks the Trolley to show a picture of when he was a baby with his mother and father. Prince Tuesday and Miss Paulificate find the picture humorous and ask to see a picture of Robert Troll as a baby, and later the Trolley also shows a picture of Miss Paulificate as a child; thus the characters are also given some background. Hamilton and the crystal ball return during the last week of the pre-hiatus shows, revealing more future scenes, including a vision of Daniel Striped Tiger married to Collette (in episode 1460).[56]

Apart from King Friday's baby picture, one of the earliest events on the Neighborhood's timeline to be shown would be the McFeelys' wedding. In episode 1476, an extended reverie shows the McFeelys' wedding, an elaborate sequence with period costumes shot in a glowing, nostalgic cinematographic style. McFeely himself narrates it, and as it ends, he comments that it was forty-five years ago; since the episode aired in 1981, this would mean that he was married in 1936 (two years before David Newell's own birth), a date further supported by the period cars and props in the sequence. McFeely, then, doesn't seem his age (he would have been supposedly in his 80s by the program's end in 2001), and relatively few of the Neighborhood of Make-Believe characters age over the course of the show, with a few exceptions, like Prince Tuesday growing from a newborn baby to a young boy. The Neighborhood does, however, receive an update in the sequel series that appeared in September 2012, *Daniel Tiger's Neighborhood*, the cast of which is made up of the children of the original neighborhood characters, moving the entire neighborhood into a later time.

Besides geography and history, world-building also occurs in the form of genealogy; characters' family trees are built up over time as new characters are revealed and discussed. King Friday XIII's father is Grandfather Thursday (presumably King Thursday), and Thursday's great-great-great-grandfather is King Monday IX. King Friday has an older sister, Claire (who is the mother of Lady Aberlin), and a younger brother, Paul; we learn in episode 1553 that he had four children: Nicky, Quentin, Polly, and Kevin. King Friday himself is married to Sara Saturday, and they have two children, Prince Tuesday and Prince Wednesday; the latter was added in *Daniel Tiger's Neighborhood*, which also added X the Owl's nephew O the Owl, Henrietta Pussycat's daughter Katerina, and Daniel Tiger, son of Daniel Striped Tiger. Other families on *Mister Rogers' Neighborhood* include Mr. and Mrs. Frogg and their son Tadpole, the Platypus family (Dr. Bill, his wife Elsie Jean, and their daughter Ana (Dr. Bill's great-great-grandfather Alexander MacKenzie MacKay is also mentioned)), and Mr. and Mrs. McFeely (whose relatives are mentioned and shown in their wedding flashback).

References to existing locations, events, and people from other episodes reward frequent and long-time viewers, and may also be things missed or misunderstood by a casual or intermittent viewer.

In episode 1517, Rogers asks whether the viewer remembers visiting Mrs. Hartman at the Neighborhood kindergarten, an event from episode 1461 which had aired almost four years earlier (though it could have been seen in reruns). In episode 1361, when Rogers is eating waffles with others, he parodies two of his songs, changing the lyrics of "It's Such a Good Feeling" to "It's such a good waffle, a very good waffle", and the lyrics of "Many Ways to Say I Love You" to "There are many ways to top a waffle". Some episodes will show clips from earlier episodes, such as episode 1703, where Barbara Smith visits; during the show, a clip is shown from her visit in episode 1010, over twenty-seven years earlier.

Other intertextual references can be noted on one viewing if they refer to texts outside of the show, such as the literary references in some character names, like Donkey Hodie (Don Quixote), or X the Owl and Henrietta Pussycat, references to Edward Lear's poem "The Owl and the Pussycat" (1871). Some names come from Rogers' own life: Daniel from Dorothy Daniel, Sara from his wife Sara Joanne, and McFeely from his grandfather, Fred Brooks McFeely. Other in-show references are more obscure; for example, the reoccurring appearance of the number 143; for example, it is seen on Lady Aberlin's fire hat in episode 1744, and in episode 1652, McFeely has a computer printout of his deliveries and tells Rogers he is number 143 on the list. In episode 1698, the meaning of the number is revealed: each number counts the letters in each word of the phrase "I love you". Rogers liked the number so much that he kept his weight consistently at 143 pounds for the last thirty years of his life.[57]

Some of the references may even require years, even decades, of familiarity with the show. For example, the Castle waterfall in episode 1490 is not seen again until episode 1741, eighteen years later (1981 to 1999), when it is given as a gift to the people of Westwood. In episode 1744, from 1999, a reference is made to the fire in Corney's factory, which occurred on the show in 1968 (episode 0063), twenty-one years earlier. No children could have possibly remembered the event, or even seen it in reruns; only parents, who had watched the show themselves as children and were now watching with their own children, could have remembered it. Rogers also had his optometrist, Dr. Bernard Mallinger, on the show in March 1968, in episode 0024, and then again over thirty years later in July 1998, in episode 1728. Letters Rogers received revealed that many parents watched the show along with their young children, so the fact that the dual audience is acknowledged should not be surprising.

The overall effect of world-building and intertextual references is to strengthen the illusion of an imaginary world and make it seem more like a real place, and thus give the events occurring there greater weight. Even in the case of fantastic characters and situations, the suggestion that the characters and places have a history (and to a certain degree, they actually did, accruing over the years that the program continued) gave more of a sense of depth to the proceedings—and for parents particularly, a sense of nostalgia, since they would be more likely to understand references to the show's past that their children would not. In the latter years of the show, and in its years in syndication afterward, many parents could remember watching the show during their own childhood, perhaps even recalling such early events as the marriage of King Friday and Queen Sara or the birth of Prince Tuesday. Parents may be more likely to encourage their own children to watch a show because of the nostalgic value it had for them, thus perpetuating the viewing of the program.

The segments of the program set in the Neighborhood of Make-Believe often contributed elements to long-term overarching narrative structures, strengthening emotional engagement and investment, and encouraging and rewarding viewers who were able to remember such events. For many viewers, the Neighborhood of Make-Believe was the heart of the program, the place where lessons were lived out in drama rather than merely discussed. And the heart of the Neighborhood, was, of course, the neighbors, the topic of the next chapter.

4 The Neighbors

A Diverse Sociological and Ontological Spectrum

Rogers was not only ahead of his time regarding the concern for diversity within children's television, but he went farther than merely race, gender, and ethnicity, creating an entire ontological spectrum of characters imbued with personality and presenting them in such a way that the assumed egalitarian world view they embodied appeared natural, as opposed to foregrounded or forced; thus, instead of being one of the show's topics, the value of diversity was an ever-present assumption on the show. And, perhaps as importantly, this inclusivity was always extended to the "television neighbor" of the viewing audience as well, who was told "You are special" and "There's no one else like you". Yet this theme of individuality never overshadowed the equally important emphasis on community, incarnated in the form of the neighborhood. Thus, the show also promoted tolerance and respect for difference, as evidenced by the many conflicts arising from differences in opinion and outlook, which were usually resolved through discussion and understanding.

Gender, Race, Ethnicity, and More

When Rogers was a child, his parents took in an older African-American boy, George Allen, to live with the family, when Allen was sixteen and Rogers was five. Allen later went on to become a jazz pianist and a flying instructor for Tuskegee airmen, and even taught Rogers how to fly a Piper Cub when he was in high school. As a guest on *The Arsenio Hall Show*, Rogers explained that growing up with Allen had a profound influence on his life.[58] This appreciation for diversity is apparent on *Mister Rogers' Neighborhood*, with its wide range of guests on the show from all walks of life, including Asians, Blacks, Hispanics, people of various ethnicities, a blind artist, children in wheelchairs, and more. Everyone was treated equally and racial differences were usually not foregrounded; it was merely assumed that, as Rogers often said, everyone was special and unique. That everyone was important and should be treated equally was simply one of the background assumptions of every episode of the program.

Rogers also had done graduate work in Child Development and consulted weekly with Dr. Margaret McFarland until her death in 1988. Dr. Albert V. Corrado was another consultant for the show until 1994; the three were the show's main research team. This situation was different from that of *Sesame Street*, which had a 45-person advisory board that met quarterly and advised on curricular issues as well as such things as the personality characteristics of minority models in the program's cast and even the level of black dialect that would appear on the program.[59] By the end of the first season, *Sesame Street* had "seven full-time formative researchers on the show, all day, every day"[60], leading to the finely honed approach to education that they took and continue to take. That the two shows can be compared despite Rogers' much smaller budget and resource base is a testament to what he was able to accomplish. The smaller team also meant Rogers had more control over the show; however, the show's heavy reliance on him also meant that it would likely not survive his retirement, which proved to be the case, unlike with *Sesame Street*, which was never heavily dependent on a single person and still continues today.

Mister Rogers' Neighborhood's main human cast members were likewise a diverse ensemble, as were its puppet characters, with a fairly equal balance of males and females in each. Rogers' own growth in sensitivity toward gender roles can also be seen over the early course of the show; as pointed out by Nina E. Lerman, Ruth Oldenziel, and Arwen P. Mohun, song lyrics from the 1960s that included gender stereotypes were rewritten by Rogers in the 1970s to remove those stereotypes.[61] There were also feminine males (like Daniel Striped Tiger) and masculine females (like Lady Elaine Fairchilde), and characters with different combinations of traits. Other characters, like Purple Panda and the Neighborhood Trolley, seemed to have little or no gender at all (although other Planet Purple citizens are named "Paul" and "Pauline"). Rogers himself represented the nurturing, sensitive male and a rejection of machismo. In addition to voicing male puppets

(King Friday XIII, Daniel Striped Tiger, X the Owl, Grandpere Tiger, Cornflake S. Pecially, Edgar Cooke, Donkey Hodie, and Ino A. Horse), Rogers also voiced several female ones (Queen Sara Saturday, Lady Elaine Fairchilde, Henrietta Pussycat, and Collette Tiger). One critic, Aram Bakshian, Jr., has even claimed that Rogers' puppets "exude androgyny".[62]

Likewise, racial and ethnic diversity were also present. The show's regular cast included Whites (Chuck Aber, Betty Aberlin, Robert Trow), Blacks (Maggie Stewart, François Clemmons, Marilyn Barnett, Ella Jenkins, Keith David),[63] Hispanics (Tony Chiroldes, Sergio Pinto, José Cisneros), and Asians (Yoshi Ito and frequent guest Yo-Yo Ma). Chiroldes (and his character, Hula Mouse), Pinto, and Cisneros spoke Spanish, while the tigers Grandpere and Collette spoke French; and Dr. Bill Platypus was Scottish (and was said to have completed his medical studies in Australia). As for the choice of animals to represent them, the latter two examples are particularly curious, when one considers that tigers are not native to France, nor is the platypus native to Scotland. And to the list of cultures appearing on the show, we might add Maggie Stewart's frequent use of sign language, an acknowledgment of the deaf community, and Purple Panda, an alien from another planet.

Regional accents, commonly used in radio shows to make character voices distinct, were also present, but were not used as caricature as they often were elsewhere; for example, X the Owl, Queen Sara, and Betty Okonak Templeton Jones all sound Southern, while Betty's husband James has a British accent. On the other hand, Ana, daughter of Dr. Bill Platypus, does not have a Scottish accent while her father does, implying a generational difference in assimilation to American culture. Considering that the show's original audience was of a generation whose parents and grandparents were immigrants, one can see that this could become a point of identification. Ana Platypus, Daniel Striped Tiger, and Prince Tuesday all attend class together at Harriet Cow's schoolhouse, where they learn and are acculturated together; Prince Tuesday's presence may even signal a crossing of class boundaries, since he is royalty while the others are commoners.

Interracial and interspecies friendships are also common on the program. Besides the various friendships between humans and puppet characters, there is the close friendship between X the Owl and Henrietta Pussycat (as mentioned, an allusion to Edward Lear's poem), even though cats and birds are often predators and prey in the wild. There is even an interracial marriage in the Neighborhood of Make-Believe, if one includes its extension in *Daniel Tiger's Neighborhood*; one of the show's characters, Elaina, is a dark-skinned girl who is the daughter of Lady Elaine Fairchilde and Music Man Stan, a black man with an afro and sideburns who runs a music shop.[64]

An interracial relationship that did appear on the show, between Maggie Stewart and Chuck Aber, attracted some notice, and was, as Betty Aberlin sees it, part of the show's celebration of blackness:

> Henrietta Pussycat was originally a black pussycat. The puppet was black. I sang a song called, "You are pretty, / You are black, / You are beautifully dressed, / Finely curled, / Perfectly you are pretty, / Elegant, you are black." She was always meant to be—as Mayor Maggie, Princess Zelda, Ella Jenkins—Mabel Mercer was on and sang two beautiful songs—was the gorgeous elegance of the black race, or what have you. Although Chuck and Maggie, who were each other's own—not only in Pittsburgh of that time, and maybe for their own reasons never actually married, but on the show they were an unstated couple. At a time when—think about the Sixties—a show that was being beamed into the South was not going to stand that. Maggie, very early on as Mayor Maggie, with Chuck as her Associate Mayor, rather than the other way around: [they] were modeling the reality that has finally come to be real.[65]

The issue of race was never used to divide people, which is perhaps the reason it was never foregrounded. To do so would draw attention away from the main message that each person is unique and should be loved, as a whole person, for who they are. While the issue of race was not ignored, neither was it discussed overtly; the very design of the show itself included tacit assumptions that made it seem strange to treat people differently due to skin color or any other physical difference. And the diversity of the program went beyond race and gender; the very nature of the characters themselves spans a broad ontological spectrum unlike any other show found on television.

A Diverse Ontological Spectrum

On the high end of the spectrum, we have human characters who play themselves: for example, Fred Rogers and all of the real-life guests on his program. Though their appearances are sometimes scripted, they are not portraying characters and only represent themselves. Then there are the human characters who portray themselves as well as fictional versions of themselves (usually in the Neighborhood of Make-Believe); Betty Aberlin/Lady Aberlin, Chuck Aber/Neighbor Aber, Joe Negri/Handyman Negri, and Maggie Stewart/Mayor Maggie. The overlap between the fictional and real identities is evident in how the names change; part of the original name is used and combined with a title indicating a role or function (an exception would be Audrey Roth/Miss Paulificate, the Castle's telephone operator). Two other humans have slightly different situations on the program; Robert Trow appears as himself in the television neighborhood, but his human character in the Neighborhood of Make-Believe, Robert Troll, is a character more stylized than the other dual characters, with relatively little of his "real" persona overlapping his make-believe one (he dresses in a troll costume and often mutters unintelligibly). Trow's other Neighborhood of Make-Believe character, the costume character Bob Dog, is even more fantastic and represents something ontologically between a human and a dog (perhaps reminiscent of the Dog-Man of *The Island of Dr. Moreau* (1896)).[66] Finally, there is David Newell's Mr. McFeely (Speedy Delivery); he and Mrs. McFeely are the only two characters who consistently appear in both the "real" world and the Neighborhood of Make-Believe.[67] Unlike all the other human cast members, they never appear as themselves (Mr. McFeely is referred to as "David" in episode 1476 and others, but is still "David McFeely"). These dual roles and their exceptions are never openly discussed or explained, yet the ontological rules they follow are consistent enough for children to learn over the course of multiple episodes.

Although at first the divide between humans and puppets seems unambiguous, one can find characters who cross over. Like Pinocchio, a puppet who becomes a real boy, *Howdy Doody* featured Princess Summerfall Winterspring of the Tinka Tonka tribe, who was first introduced as a puppet, then later was transformed into a real, live princess, played by Judy Tyler. In the Neighborhood of Make-Believe, Rogers adds his own twist, by having Lady Aberlin be the niece of King Friday XIII. As we discover in episode 1553, King Friday's older sister Claire is Lady Aberlin's mother, making Lady Aberlin half-puppet, half-human, rather than wholly one or the other, giving her a rather unique ontological status different from even characters like

Pinocchio or Princess Winterspring, whose ontological status merely changes from one to the other. Other than being called a niece to King Friday and a cousin to Prince Tuesday, however, her status is not discussed, leaving the details of the inferred human-puppet union to the imagination.[68] Two other minor characters, who are cousins of X the Owl, Cousin Mary Owl and Cousin Stephen Owl, are costume characters played by humans, with human faces surrounded by feathers, implying something ontologically between bird and human (which, again, raises questions regarding their origins).

Next, there are the puppet characters that are designed to look like humans, like King Friday, Queen Sara, Prince Tuesday, Edgar Cooke, Lady Elaine, and others. Some of these, however, are slightly more abstract in their design, like Betty Okonak Templeton Jones and her husband James, whose heads are of soft cloth. Beyond them are animal puppets that are anthropomorphic to varying degrees. Cornflake S. Pecially is quite close to a human (puppet), speaking like one, dressing in a suit, and working in his own factory. Likewise, Dr. Bill Platypus is fully dressed and has a university education and a medical practice. Henrietta Pussycat is fully clothed, but her English is fractured, with "meow" replacing many words. Daniel Striped Tiger's English is good, but he usually wears only a wristwatch, and X the Owl has only his feathers for clothing. There are also the life-sized puppets that are costume characters, like Bob Dog and Purple Panda (and, visiting on one episode, Big Bird). Finally, there are animal puppets with little or no anthropomorphic design, like Old Goat, who does not wear clothes and does not speak English, communicating what little he does through varying "Maaa" sounds, which others interpret. We could also include here, perhaps ahead of the nonanthropomorphic puppets, the real animals appearing on the show, like Rogers' fish and Robert Trow's dog.

Further down the spectrum are puppets that are controlled by other puppets, what we might call diegetic puppets, which have no autonomy of their own (likewise, we can also find costume characters playing other costume characters, as in episode 1470, when the dinosaur seen in the Neighborhood turns out to be Purple Panda in a costume). An example of diegetic puppets can be found in episode 1550 (see Figure 4.1); during the Bass Violin Festival in Southwood, the puppet James Michael Jones and the human character Keith David put on a puppet show with talking bass violin puppets that they control: Jimmy Bass Violin and Keith Bass Violin, respectively. James's wife Betty comments on how

Figure 4.1 Betty Okonak Templeton Jones comments on how real the bass violin puppets have become to her (top, left): James Michael Jones and Keith David display the bass violin puppets (top, right); a close-up of the bass violin puppets (bottom, left); and Daniel talking to Jimmy Bass Violin (bottom, right).

real the bass violin puppets have become to her (in episode 1548), and during the puppet show, Daniel feels the sorrow that Jimmy Bass Violin is experiencing and begins consoling the puppet, forgetting that it is not real, and then feels strange afterward when he is reminded that it is not real. Thus, in addition to having a puppet-show-within-a-puppet-show, we also have a puppet character (Daniel) to whom the human characters talk as if he were a real person, who is reminded that the diegetic puppet character which he started to talk to and take for a real person was in fact not real; and this entire situation itself occurs in the Neighborhood of Make-Believe within *Mister Rogers' Neighborhood*. Such nested diegeses and multiple levels of realism demonstrate the complexity, and blend of fantasy and reality, that is often overlooked or left unacknowledged in analyses or discussions of *Mister Rogers' Neighborhood*. Another example of a nested diegesis occurs in episode

1384, which takes viewers behind the scenes to demonstrate how Rogers' show is made; in the Neighborhood of Make-Believe segment of the episode, Lady Elaine starts her own TV station at the Museum-Go-Round, MGR-TV (and is making her own shows by episode 1387), resulting in a diegetic TV studio making a show on a set within a real TV studio making a show. And in episode 1390, Henrietta controls a witch puppet on Lady Elaine's TV show, resulting in a puppet controlling a puppet on a TV show within a TV show.

A similar situation occurs in the show's operas, where Neighborhood of Make-Believe characters play roles, some of which involve portraying characters who are ontologically different than themselves. Thus we have Lady Aberlin and Donkey Hodie cast as mother and son in the "Babysitter" opera in episode 0045, and Don Brockett, Audrey Roth, and Betty Aberlin all playing talking cats in "A Star for Kitty" (episode 1565), which also features various human and puppet characters in costumed roles as half-moons (John Reardon and Paul Spencer Adkins) and stars (Chuck Aber, Daniel Striped Tiger, Lady Elaine, James Michael Jones, and Cornflake S. Pecially), both of which are otherwise inanimate objects. The opera's characters are also cast to match, to some degree, the personalities of the human characters and puppets as they normally appear on the show; for example, Daniel's characters are shy and timid, while Lady Elaine's are more outspoken. And the show-within-a-show idea is even carried another level deeper; "Windstorm in Bubbleland" (episode 1475) features a television news show within its operatic story, which makes it a television-show-within-an-opera-within-a-television-show.

Finally, at the low end of the ontological spectrum, we find inanimate objects which appear to be sentient, like the Neighborhood Trolley, the "Express de Grandparents" trolley, or King Friday's wooden birds on sticks, Mimus Polyglottus and Troglodytes Aedon. The Neighborhood Trolley moves back and forth by itself and chimes to talk (people interpret what it is saying), while the wooden birds on sticks move around by themselves (with no attempt made to hide the sticks), and King Friday addresses them as though they can understand him. One of the wooden birds on a stick, Mimus Polyglottos, even plays a part as a policebird in "As the Museum Turns" in episode 1665. Occasionally we find a few other objects that seem to have agency, like the kite in episode 1021 or the rocking horse that flies away in episode 1557. Prince Tuesday also has Tome the Ragdoll, who comes to life in five episodes (1622, 1623, 1637, 1648, and 1649) and is played by human actor Tome Cousin. Lastly, at the very end of the spectrum, we might include Malcolm Apricot Dinko, Daniel Striped Tiger's imaginary friend from episode 1649.

The puppets on *Mister Rogers' Neighborhood* are also noticeably different in style from the Muppets of *Sesame Street*. While some of the softer, cloth puppets have mouths that move, like the Muppets, many of Rogers' puppets, especially the older ones who are the more regular cast members, are an older style of puppet with no moving eyes or mouths, and with arms incapable of doing very much. Gus Allegretti, the main puppeteer for *Captain Kangaroo*, reflected on the differences in puppets and how children relate to them:

> Because the difficulty of moving gracefully or picking things up was something they (the children) understood; I mean they ("old" puppets) were more like them (the children) in that kind of behavior than not. And then when they ("old" puppets) weren't quite real, which was kind of the magic, if you will, there was that special charm … When the "new" puppets came in … they removed some of that connection and they removed that separateness too that distinguished a puppet and a child and made the puppet more like a child.[69]

Just as he explained the studio and Trolley, Rogers also took time in the show to demystify the puppets, showing them to the audience in his television house and explaining how he controls them and gives them a voice. He did this on multiple occasions, including episodes 1384, 1689, and 1726. Likewise, Rogers also demonstrated that the costume characters had people inside them. When Caroll Spinney's Big Bird was going to appear on the show, Rogers wanted him to reveal that Big Bird was someone in costume, but Spinney refused, saying he did not want to destroy the illusion of Big Bird. They reached a compromise, and Big Bird appeared on episode 1483. According to the Muppet Wiki,

> Caroll Spinney agreed to appear in the episode as Big Bird after some dialogue with Fred Rogers; when Spinney originally received the script for the show he saw it required him to remove the costume and discuss the inner-workings of the Big Bird puppet.

Spinney protested, as he didn't believe in ruining the illusion of Big Bird for the children. Rogers agreed, but only under the stipulation that Big Bird's appearance was restricted to the fantasy segments of the "Neighborhood of Make-Believe", as he didn't believe in perpetuating the deceitful blur of real and pretend to children that occurred when presenting the character as real in the "real world".

While *Sesame Street Unpaved* mentions that Rogers understood Spinney's concern over showing the children how Big Bird works, Spinney said at some of his book signings (promoting his autobiography, *The Wisdom of Big Bird*) that he and Fred Rogers argued over the phone for roughly twenty minutes over whether or not to have him tell the kids how he performs Big Bird.

In the same episode, Rogers still throws a disguised punch back at Spinney by putting on a tall giraffe costume shortly before Big Bird's appearance, stating to the child viewer "When you see big make-believe creatures in parades or in plays or on television, you can know that the people inside are just pretending to be something else". He adds "Sometimes of course there are machines inside of them too, that make them move. But they're just pretend".[70]

The image of Mister Rogers arguing for twenty minutes with the man behind Big Bird shows that Rogers himself was not immune to conflict, and interpersonal conflict, along with its resolution, was a frequent theme for Neighborhood of Make-Believe segments of the program.

A Neighbor Just Like You: Interpersonal Conflict and Resolution

If you've watched Mister Rogers' Neighborhood, *you probably know that our programs do not try to avoid anxiety-arousing situations. We have dealt with the beginnings of life, as well as with its end, and with many of the feelings in between. We do try, though, to keep anxiety within a child's manageable limits and then to deal with it. We talk about those feelings and, in simple ways, try to show models for coping with them as well as models of trustworthy, caring, and available adults.*

Fred Rogers[71]

Mister Rogers' Neighborhood and its Neighborhood of Make-Believe are by no means as utopic in their composition as some critics might think; interpersonal problems and conflicts regularly occurred within the diegesis and had to be resolved, occasionally even on a larger scale; in 1983, during the episodes on conflict (1521–1525), King Friday orders the making of bombs in the Neighborhood of Make-Believe when it is believed that Southwood might be going to war with them, bringing a touch of Cold War anxiety to the Neighborhood. Rogers' show was also unique in that problems were not neatly solved at the end of every episode; sometimes it took all five episodes in a week-long storyline for a conflict to be resolved. And some issues, like divorce, are simply dealt with as they are; as Kimmel and Collins write,

> The truth is Mister Rogers never said the world was always safe, always sunny, always a good place. A quick review of the roster of *Neighborhood* themes—death, divorce, strife between friends—is anything but jolly, nor were the resolutions always neat. In one episode, Neighbor Aber has a reluctant conversation with Prince Tuesday about his divorce and the fact that he misses his children. At the end of the program, Neighbor Aber is more willing to talk about his feelings—but he and his wife are still divorced and he still misses his children. No *deus ex machina* descends to repair his marriage.[72]

In episode 1476, Prince Tuesday also meets Patty and her mother, Krista Jayne Bacardi, who is divorced, making her probably the only divorced puppet to appear on children's television. Interestingly, while most of the other post-hiatus programs name the week's theme in the opening titles, the five programs of the "Divorce" week do not.

Rogers knew that children learned best by watching how others interact, and watching how people talk through situations. Conflicts typically occurred between the puppet characters, with the human characters acting as mediators and helping to reconcile the conflicting parties. Occasionally, though, even the human characters become exasperated with others. In the first week of episodes, for example, King Friday drafts people into a border guard, sets up punch clocks to be used by people as they go place to place, and requires people to provide so much information before they can visit the Castle that Cornflake S. Pecially decides not to go instead (episode 0003), and even Lady

Aberlin sings "It's an Ugly Day" in response to her frustration with all the new regulations.

As mentioned earlier, the conflicts typically revolve around a personality conflict, selfishness, misunderstanding, or a character's plan or scheme (usually gone awry). Two of the most frequent causes of personality conflict are the often-pompous authority figure, King Friday, and his opposite, the eccentric, irreverent iconoclast, Lady Elaine Fairchilde (see Figure 4.2). While King Friday's assumptions and the proclamations based on them cause conflict (as in the two examples above), Lady Elaine usually causes it through her mischief-making. For example, in episodes 0030, 0067, 0100, and 0114, Lady Elaine uses her boomerang to turn the Neighborhood upside-down, disturbing the other residents (see Figure 4.2). In episode 0027, she takes Edgar Cooke's soft pillow away, until Nurse Miller (a human character who only appeared during the first four seasons) settles the dispute. Both characters represent the tendencies of children (and, really, all human

Figure 4.2 King Friday XIII and Lady Elaine Fairchilde seen together in episode 1506 (top, left); Lady Elaine turns the Eiffel Tower upside-down in episode 1692 (top, right); King Friday and a sign proclaiming his "No Play" rule in episode 1489 (bottom, left); and in episode 1022, a magic kite tells the arguing neighbors to "Take Turns" (bottom, right).

beings) to want to have things their way (King Friday) and to be selfish and self-centered at times (Lady Elaine).

Other conflicts arise from selfishness or a lack of sharing; for example, in episode 1022, the characters disagree as to who should be able to keep a magic kite found in the Neighborhood (until the kite shows them a message on its side, "Take Turns", see Figure 4.2). Another example occurs in episode 1506; Lady Elaine demands that Ana share her special shoes, and when Ana declines, Lady Elaine goes to complain to King Friday (iconoclast though she is, she still turns to the King as an authority figure when she thinks she is being denied justice). While it is usually the children who most need to learn to share, sometimes the children are depicted as generous and sensible as well. During the episodes on Work (1526–1530), the Neighborhood of Make-Believe Annual Report reveals a surplus of 3,000 (currency units are usually left unspecified), and King Friday decides to build a Neighborhood pool with the money. While the hole for the pool is being dug, water pipes break and are in need of repair, which is costly. While Lady Elaine suggests selling the Castle to raise the money, it is the school children who suggest using the 3,000 to fix the pipes, a proposal the King Friday finally adopts.

Misunderstandings are another source of conflict in the Neighborhood. These can typically be divided into two types: misunderstandings between friends in which a wrong assumption occurs, or the anxieties of the child characters due their inexperience with the world. The latter mostly involve Daniel, Tuesday, and Ana, who often later discuss their experiences together in the schoolhouse. Some of these experiences have to do with language, as in episode 1544, when Daniel thinks that being a ring-bearer at a wedding will mean he has to wear a bear costume, or in episode 1591 when King Friday berates Miss Paulificate for bringing garden *hoes* instead of a garden *hose*. Other misunderstandings arise from anxieties occurring in familial situations, as in episode 1517, when Prince Tuesday's feelings are hurt when his parents leave him at home in day care when they go on a trip, or in episode 1477, when he fears his parents may be getting a divorce, a fear that is not resolved until episode 1479.

Misunderstandings between friends happen often between X the Owl and Henrietta Pussycat, such as when Henrietta becomes jealous when X gives attention to Big Bird's visit in episode 1483, until she realizes that his visit will not affect her friendship with X. In episode

1576, X insults Audrey Duck when he mistakes her for Henrietta wearing "a funny duck costume". In episode 1597, Chuck Aber gives Lady Elaine a balloon ring, which leads her to believe that the two of them will get married. And in episode 1509, Lady Aberlin promises to bring Daniel to the picnic at the Castle, and he becomes upset when she forgets about him. Some misunderstandings take several episodes to be resolved, but the entire process of reconciliation is usually shown and discussed. Usually the human characters end up advising, comforting, and reconciling the puppet characters, though in rare occasions the reverse can happen (as in episode 1548, where Daniel ends up giving advice to Lady Aberlin and comforting her).

Finally, characters' plans or schemes often lead to conflict. During the "Discipline" week episodes (1491–1495), Corney produces King Friday dolls at his factory; Lady Elaine, jealous that the dolls do not look like her, takes them and alters them to look like her, and is later punished by having to work two days at the factory. In episodes 1704–05, all the vacuum sweepers are discovered to be missing, and then later found at the Museum-Go-Round, when Lady Elaine finally admits she is afraid of them. Conflict can also arise from the abuse of authority, as in episodes 1561–1565, when King Friday orders the celebration of the coming of his comet, without realizing that not everyone wants to celebrate and that a comet cannot be owned. In episodes 1671–1675, King Friday orders everyone in the Neighborhood to wear three-cornered hats (not surprisingly, Lady Elaine alone refuses). In episode 1487, King Friday makes a "No Play" rule (see Figure 4.2), thinking that this will help everyone avoid accidents; upset, Lady Elaine Fairchilde moves the Museum-Go-Round away to a park, and in the following episode, children set up a playground in the Museum's former location in protest against the rule, with even Prince Tuesday telling his father that people have to play. Finally, in episode 1489, struck by the fact that his "No Play" rule prohibits his own fanfare from being played, Friday relents and allows play in the Neighborhood once again.

The interpersonal conflicts in the Neighborhood of Make-Believe always end with forgiveness and reconciliation, and the feelings of parties on both sides of the conflict are carefully considered and discussed, including the process of conflict resolution. An understanding is reached on both sides, preventing both retaliation and humiliation, and both sides learn something from the situation.

While the details of the situations are often whimsical, all the fears, failings, and weaknesses that the characters exhibit are real and common enough for children to connect to their own lives. Special episodes have also dealt with special topics. According to Donna Mitroff and Rebecca Herr Stephenson,

Early in the life of the show, Fred Rogers' deep concern for children led him to create a special episode of the [show] in reaction to the 1968 assassination of Robert F. Kennedy (Rogers, 1968). The episode, which Rogers wrote overnight, was broadcast a few days following the incident and was shown in the evening to ensure parents' ability to watch with their children. The episode alternates between Rogers talking directly to parents (in the same way that he talks directly to child viewers) in the living room of his television house and a dramatization in the Land of Make-Believe. The vignettes in the Land of Make-Believe work to illustrate the power of play for children in understanding and expressing feelings about upsetting situations. […]

Sensitive subjects are regularly discussed on the show within the context of the Land of Make-Believe. This particular episode incorporates a second layer of fantasy, as the characters in the Land of Make-Believe pretend to reenact the assassination shown on television. Anxieties manifest in a variety of ways, ranging from Daniel Striped Tiger's generalized fears for his own safety to the anxieties that surface for X the Owl and Lady Elaine Fairchild [*sic*] due to their misunderstanding of the differences between pretending or wishing that something will happen, and acting in a way to carry out the action. Exchanges between the human (adult) and puppet (child) characters in the Land of Make-Believe model coping and communication skills for children and parents alike. Additionally, this special episode contains segments intended specifically for parents. In these segments, Rogers attempted to help parents understand their roles in helping children deal with violent events, as well as the emotions leading to and surrounding violent actions. In this way, Rogers both taught coping skills and developed strategies for resiliency. In addition to having discussed and modeled these strategies, Rogers expressed his concern with graphic displays of violence on television, and issued a plea for parents to protect their children from such images.[73]

Likewise, in 1981, Rogers did another special episode, "Violence in the News: Helping Children Understand", due to the shootings and assassination attempts in the news that year.

Even in the regular episodes, often when the Neighborhood of Make-Believe segment ends, Rogers adds further summary and explanation after the Trolley returns to the television house. For example, in episode 1506, Lady Elaine wants Ana to share her special shoes, and King Friday and other characters calmly explain that sometimes people have special things they shouldn't have to share, and ask if she has things she doesn't want to share, which she reluctantly admits. Afterward the segment ends and the Trolley returns, Rogers says,

> Sharing is hard sometimes for everyone, isn't it? Everybody has some things that they shouldn't have to share. Do you have a blanket, or a stuffed animal, or a pillow? Well, if it's extra special to you, that's something you shouldn't have to share.

This dual-pronged approach, involving direct talk about a topic as well as illustrative examples played out as drama, makes Rogers and his program especially effective at getting across his messages, which is also the topic of the following chapter.

5 "And I'll Have More Ideas for You"

Ideology and the Neighborhood

"You are special." It is a cliché that has brought Fred Rogers national acclaim—and a deceptively simple lesson in self-esteem. It is rooted in religion, in a spiritual quest, in an identifiable philosophy. The philosophy has to do with the human urge to create.

J. M. Laskas, "The Gospel According to Fred Rogers"[74]

Until change comes from within the industry, television will continue to have a negative effect on children, family life, and human relationships in general. Often, the kindest thing one can say about a television program these days is that it is a waste of time. Much of television, though, is degrading, reducing important human feelings to the status of caricatures or trivia. Some of it, in my opinion, even encourages pathology. Yet here it is, for hours a day, part of the intimacy of family life, an influence on family values, a growing part of family tradition, and an accessory of family education. We parents need to think hard about how television is affecting our children and in turn, our grandchildren to come. We need to think harder still about what to do about it.

Fred Rogers[75]

Mister Rogers' Neighborhood is one of those rare programs accepted and appreciated by people on both sides of the political divisions we find in society today, like those of conservative/liberal, Republican/Democrat, right/left, and so on. Yet neither the program nor Rogers himself are neutral on the same issues which divide Americans into these diametrically opposed groups, nor can Rogers be placed neatly into the camps on either side. *Mister Rogers' Neighborhood* stood out for the messages it contained for children and any adults who might be watching; in an interview with researcher Lucille Burbank, Rogers mentioned that he had received letters from adults responding to the show's message that "You are worthwhile".[76] Even Sam Newbury, the supervising producer of *Mister Rogers' Neighborhood*, admitted,

> I think that's why certain books remain classics. They touch something in us that we need to go over again or learn about again, and I think in certain ways *Mister Rogers' Neighborhood* does that if you allow it to. Children are much more able to allow it than adults are, but it's a very powerful show because it reaches very powerful parts of you. I think even as an adult I'm often surprised at how emotionally touched I am by the subject of the show and by the shows themselves.[77]

In the Introduction to his book *Dear Mister Rogers, Does It Ever Rain in Your Neighborhood?: Letters to Mister Rogers*, Rogers mentions that

> lately, at least once a day, we hear from teenagers and young adults who tell us that even now they stop and look at our program and want us to know how much our Neighborhood visits mean to them as they were growing up.[78]

For many, the show is something that continues to influence one even into adulthood, and adult fans can also be quite protective of the show as well. While there are relatively few academic or even journalistic essays directly critical of Rogers, occasionally one appears. On July 5, 2007, Jeffrey Zaslow's *Wall Street Journal* article "Blame It on Mr. Rogers: Why Young Adults Feel So Entitled" argued that Rogers' message of "You are special" encouraged feelings of entitlement in an entire generation, quoting Don Chance, a finance professor at Louisiana State University, who had written about Rogers.[79] The essay ignited a firestorm of angry replies, led to a Fox News segment, and finally a response from Chance himself who felt his initial statements had been misrepresented, in which he wrote,

> I did respond to reporters in those few days afterwards. I did no formal interviews but answered a few questions. It was also quite interesting that Fox News originally reported my story as being a

"professor at Louisiana State University [who] did this study that showed that Mr. Rogers had damaged generations of children". I can certainly see that this would have been a headline-grabbing story, but of course, no such study was ever done. I sent an explanatory note that was read on Fox & Friends. Here is the text:

I made a casual observation that we have a society full of people who think they're entitled to things they haven't earned. The reference to Rogers was just a metaphor. As the article says, he is representative of a culture of excessive doting but he is not the problem itself. That said, it was just an observation. I have no professional qualifications to evaluate the real problems or propose solutions. Mr. Rogers was a great American. I watched him with my children and wouldn't hesitate to do so again if I had young children. I would just want to make sure that they know that people become special by the choices they make, not by who they are and that the world owes you nothing.

Then in the manner of a raging forest fire, the internet grapevine reported that I had apologized and backed off. There was truly nothing to apologize for and I certainly did not back off. I think the above statement is clear. I just explained my position.[80]

While it may be an exaggeration to blame the culture of entitlement on Rogers or his program, it is interesting that some of the responses he received missed the point and were so angry that Chance was prompted to also write, "It was, after all, an off-hand metaphorical comment, for which I paid a heavy price in the vitriol I received from fans of Mr. Rogers, many of whom clearly did not get his message about how to treat people".[81]

Rogers' emphasis on personal value should not be conflated with the failed self-esteem movement in 1990s education, which included such things as the "I Love Me" sessions that schoolchildren were forced to endure in certain California schools.[82] Rogers' approach was subtler, more nuanced, and less insistent, and he balanced his message by keeping others in mind; the community was never allowed to be eclipsed by the individual or any form of egotism. While Neighborhood characters occasionally fell prey to self-centeredness, they would soon be corrected by the rest of the community, albeit in a calm and loving fashion.

Likewise, Rogers was careful about the way his faith appeared on the show. As an ordained Presbyterian minister who attended an Episcopal church, met the Dalai Lama, was a close friend and student of Catholic priest and author Henri Nouwen, and who grew up near a Benedictine monastery (which later named a center after him), Fred Rogers was a Christian who was aware of multiple denominational traditions.[83] Following one of his favorite[84] quotations (attributed to St. Francis of Assisi), "Preach the Gospel at all times, when necessary use words", Rogers was able to advance his Christian beliefs on his show partly because many (though not all) of the principles advanced were universal ones as well ("Love your neighbor", "Share with others", "Respect others", "Recycle", etc.). The show's audience included children of all faiths and backgrounds, with values that extended beyond any single world view, and it was those principles shared by multiple faiths that were emphasized the most.

There are a few episodes of Rogers' show that have overt religious references; in episode 1476, God is mentioned by the minister performing the McFeelys' wedding, and in the early days of the show, God was mentioned more overtly. In episode 0015, Rogers and Vivian Richman sing "This Little Light of Mine" and "He's Got the Whole World in His Hands", and in episodes 0005, 0029, and 0120, Rogers sang his own song, "Goodnight, God", which he had also used on *The Children's Corner*.[85] One song, the "Creation Duet", mentions God in its lyrics several times when it is sung in episode 0041 in 1968; but when the song is used again in 1985 (in episode 1636), the word "God" is replaced with the word "Love", an example of the encroaching secularization present even in Rogers' show. Finally, in episode 1525, the week-long discussion of conflict ends with text of Isaiah 2:4 displayed on-screen before the end credits. Most of the time, however, the show's messages are usually advanced through more generalized ideas and the way those ideas are presented; much of this relies on the show's contemplative nature.

Slowness, Silence, and Reflection

The slow pace of Rogers' show promotes calm, collected thought, and moments of silence encourage reflection. In a world of cell phones, iPods, and constant noise and disruption, silence is feared and considered "dead air time", and is increasingly rare in people's lives, even children's, making Rogers' show stand out in the culture even more today than it did when it first aired. Such a change of pace is so alien to some adults that in 1985 one critic, Aram Bakshian Jr., called the show "overpoweringly dull", writing,

> The premise of the show, shaped in part by two "psychological consultants" whose names are run with the credits, seems to be that hyperactive young Americans need nothing so much as a daily aerial lobotomy, presided over by an unmenacing Ma-Bap [*sic*] figure embodying the virtues of a kindly granddad and a particularly unassertive schoolmarm. Maybe they're right, given the flood of animated monster tales, mindless shootouts, and car chases that most kids choose when viewing commercial programming.[86]

Apart from Bakshian's reluctant admission that "maybe they're right", Bakshian seems to miss the point of the show's radically different pace as a refuge from the surrounding culture's noise and acceleration. As Rogers said in an interview,

> I just feel there isn't enough silence, you know, and I'm always asking people if they can just give some silence. And we're in a medium that allows so little of that. The last time I was at the White House, I said, "Would you please just have a half-minute of silence to think about somebody who has helped you become who you are?" and that whole fancy meeting, you know, that whole fancy East Room of the White House, sitting silently, thinking about people who they might not have thought of for a long time that had made a big difference in their lives.[87]

Rogers called for a similar moment of silence in his acceptance speech for the Lifetime Achievement Award at the 24th Annual Daytime Emmy Awards in 1997, but (perhaps due to the audience being made up of members of the television industry) limited the time to only ten seconds.[88]

Rogers' slow speaking style was not just to calm his audience, but by all accounts was how he spoke most of the time, as one can see in Rogers' interview footage, acceptance speeches, and even his congressional testimony. The slow rate allows Rogers, and his audience, whoever they may be, to listen and reflect as he speaks. As Hollingsworth writes,

Fred Rogers was one of those who was very far advanced in the Lord's service and who often employed the prayer of silence. It wasn't just the absence of noise that he advocated, but silence that reflects on the goodness of God, the goodness of what and whom He made. Silence to think about those who have helped us. He knew that silence leads to reflection, that reflection leads to appreciation, and that appreciation looks about for someone to thank: "I trust that they will thank God, for it is God who inspires and informs all that is nourishing and good", he once said.[89]

Another reason for Rogers' careful, serene pace was his respect for others and his willingness to give them his time and attention, something Rogers did because he looked for, and found, the value in others.

Finding the Value in Others

In researching what Fred Rogers was really like, one thing comes up over and over: "What you see is what you get". Those who knew him say that he was just as you see him on the show: kind, considerate, caring, a good listener, and truly interested in other people. Those who wrote to him received a personal reply, and authors and filmmakers who interviewed him for a project often began lifelong friendships with Rogers.[90] Asked what would his single most important message be if he had one final broadcast to make, Rogers replied,

Well, I would want [those] who were listening somehow to know that they had unique value, that there isn't anybody in the whole world exactly like them and that there never has been and never will be.

And that they are loved by the Person who created them, in a unique way.

If they could know that and really know it and have that behind their eyes, they could look with those eyes on their neighbor and realize, "My neighbor has unique value too; there's never been anybody in the whole world like my neighbor, and there never will be". If they could value that person—if they could love that person—in ways that we know the Eternal loves us, then I would be very grateful.[91]

Today one rarely finds the combination of (or at least the degree of) sweetness and sincerity that one finds on Rogers' show, which is completely lacking in humor that even slightly demeans others. Even adults who worked on the show did not remain unaffected by the show's outlook. Actress Betty Aberlin, by her own account, was a cynical New Yorker who gradually came to see the wisdom of the show:

> [At first,] I thought that was just complete poppycock—"Come on, what is this 'Neighborhood'? Say hello to the postman, and 'Hi, Mr. So-and-So, how are you doing?'" I just thought, "Right. That's a *Good Housekeeping* kind of thing, come on." Because I came from New York, where if somebody says, "How are you doing", you think, "What do they mean by that?" And then years later, I realized I was the one with the skewed reality. That I had been inculcated with a sense of mistrust and danger, because that's what the city was, when I navigated it all by myself.[92]

The ability to see the value in others, no matter how different they are from you, is at the heart of Rogers' message, and part of the Judeo-Christian mandate to "Love your neighbor as yourself", a possible source of Rogers' much-beloved term for others and his connection of loving others to one's own self-esteem. Rogers introduced both ideas to children on his show through frequent messages concerning self-esteem ("You are special", "People can love you just the way you are", "Everybody's fancy") and through scenes of interpersonal communication and interaction where caring for others is modeled. As Chapter 4 has shown, that does not mean conflict was avoided, but rather that it was shown and analyzed, and also used to show how reconciliation can occur.

When it first appeared, Rogers' combination of lessons in the affective domain and the cognitive domain was unique on television. Like many other shows, *Sesame Street* in its early years took a different approach to the teaching of values. According to *Sesame Street* co-creator Joan Cooney:

> We talked about values and it was at a very difficult period in American race relations, no more difficult than now, but it was different. And there was a great deal of whose values and what are you talking about? White middle-class values? and etc. So, we decided that we would steer clear of talking about values, per se.

> We knew that we were going to teach—the children were going to demonstrate kindness to one another, recognition of differences, but we didn't try to quantify … at the time. … we knew the Office of Education was not really interested in affective [education]. We did not try to "beat" it down into curriculum that year … our main concern was in cognitive development.[93]

As Lesser and Schneider have shown, *Sesame Street* did include prosocial and affective material, even in its first season, in such areas as justice and fair play, and over the years the curriculum expanded to include Latino-American culture (season 3, 1971–2), self-esteem and the entering of social groups (season 5, 1973–4), ethnic diversity in New York City (season 10, 1978–9), and race relations between five races (seasons 22–5, 1990–4), and more.[94] Although Rogers was less overt in his discussions of such things, many of them were present on his show from early on, at least in the background.

Rogers broadened the reach of his program by mainly concentrating on values which were more universally accepted, allowing his program to find success across such a broad demographic and generational spectrum. Not only that, but the idea that everyone has value is not limited to a particular philosophical outlook; instead, it actually places a value on each person regardless of their outlook, and on their feelings as well, something which many ideologies, partisan in their outlook, do not encourage.

In 1969, testifying before the US Senate Subcommittee on Communication in support of a $20 million grant for public television that was in question, Rogers explained what his show offered;

> This is what I give; I give an expression of care, every day, to each child, to help him realize that he is unique. I end the program by saying, "You've made this day a special day, by just by your being you. There's no person in the whole world like you, and I like you just the way you are." And I feel that if we in public television can only make it clear that feelings are mentionable, and manageable, we will have done a great service for mental health.[95]

Even committee chair Senator John Pastore, known for his brusqueness, was impressed with Rogers' testimony, and concluded by saying "I think it's wonderful. … Looks like you just earned the twenty million dollars".

Fred Rogers' humility and simplicity are not just a part of the show's message, but also a reason for its continuing success. According to an article in *The Cincinnati Enquirer* by John Kiesewetter,

> Mr. Rogers' modesty "may be part of why he's lasted this long", says Sam Newbury, production director and 18-year employee. "(Fame) is not his interest. His interest is his work with children, and his faith."[96]

Rogers knew and understood his audience, and even suggested that parents who watched the show would have more empathy for children.[97] Painful experiences from his own childhood helped him to remember what it was like to be child, with the fears, worries, and vulnerability that come with childhood, but at the same time, all the joys, wonder, and freshness of vision that represent the best aspects of being a child.

Freshness of Vision: Through the Eyes of a Child

> *I would like to recapture that freshness of vision which is characteristic of extreme youth when all the world is new to it.*
> Henri Matisse, painter[98]

The content of *Mister Rogers' Neighborhood* also reflects Rogers' philosophy regarding the way children learn and become enriched, well-rounded individuals. This can be seen in the show's introduction of cultural content, as well as the discussion of issues and ideas which would most concern young children. Rogers positioned issues and ideas from the perspective of children, taking into consideration how they see the world, with a corresponding attitude that sought to treat them respectfully as individuals without condescension or pandering and without avoiding more difficult issues like anger, divorce, war, death, and the existence of Santa Claus.

Right from the start, long before the show took on its final form in the post-hiatus years, Rogers already included a healthy helping of music, art, and culture. In 1968 alone, the program's first year, episodes featured a string quartet playing music by Haydn (episode 0029); Bach cello music (0030); a tuba demonstration (0034); Bernard Goldberg's flute performance (0042); ballet (0033); needlepoint (0041); chalk drawings (0037 and 0061); opera singer John Reardon performing songs from Mozart's *The Magic Flute* (0043); Winslow Homer paintings (0061); tap dancing (0049); a mime (0051); marionettes (0057 and 0126); gymnastics and tumbling (0065); music played on a synthesizer (0068), which was cutting edge for 1968; bagpipes (0099); a poem by Robert Louis Stevenson (0103); glass blowing (0070); an electric guitar, amplifier, and the "teenage music" of Johnny Lively (0077); Van Cliburn on piano (0111); African folk music (0077); and even performing bears (0112).

With the change to themed, week-long continuities in the post-hiatus years, music, art, and culture would continue to be an important part of the show, with entire weeks devoted to topics pertaining to children's needs (see the episode list at the back of this book). These shows also brought in professionals from various fields as guests to demonstrate what they do for a living. As Rogers said in an interview,

> The best teacher in the world is somebody who loves what he or she does, and just loves it in front of you. And that's what I like to do with the Neighborhood. I love to have guests and present a whole smorgasbord of ways for the children to choose; I mean, some child might choose painting, some child might choose playing the cello, but there are so many ways of saying who we are and how we feel, ways that don't hurt anybody.[99]

And Rogers was a musician himself; he wrote and performed over 200 songs for his show, which ranged from didactical to purely whimsical. On a larger scale, there were also Rogers' operas, which also combined whimsy and surreal imagery with ideas and messages. For example, we might consider episode 1475, also known as *Windstorm in Bubbleland*, the end of a five-day series entitled "Mister Rogers Makes an Opera" (see Figure 5.1).

Windstorm in Bubbleland begins with a news report from Robert Redgate (played by John Reardon), who sings that there is "never any trouble here in Bubbleland". He also reports that the National Bubble Chemical Company has invented "spray sweaters" to protect bubbles. The newscast is suddenly interrupted by Lady Aberlin, playing the manager of Betty's Better Sweater Company, who calls the spray sweaters a fraud, saying the cans are nothing but air. Next, a dolphin named Friendly Frank (played by François Clemmons) delivers a weather report claiming the weather is perfect in Bubbleland. This report is

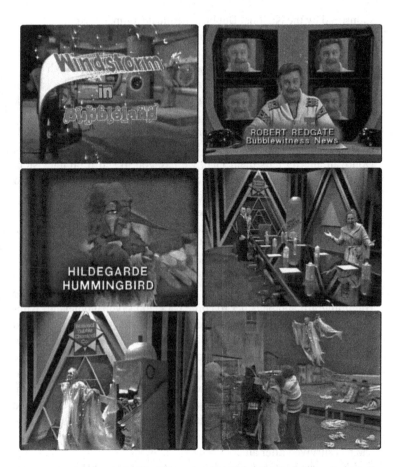

Figure 5.1 Scenes from *Windstorm in Bubbleland*: title screen (top, left); Redgate's newscast (top, right); Lady Elaine as Hildegarde Hummingbird (center, left); Donovan's office (center, right); Donovan's true identity revealed (bottom, left); and the windstorm at the docks (bottom, right). The entire opera can be viewed at pbskids.org.

interrupted by Hildegarde Hummingbird (played by Lady Elaine Fairchilde), who says that a windstorm is coming, a natural threat to bubbles. She is immediately censored and told "don't ever mention the word 'windstorm'", and the end of the newscast reveals that it is sponsored by the National Bubble Chemical Company. Not allowed to speak the truth, Hildegarde Hummingbird leaves Bubbleland.

At the docks, a Banana Boat Imports boat captain (played by Don Brockett) and a bubble vendor (played by Miss Paulificate) both notice that the air is strange and there are more waves at sea. The captain criticizes Frank for not reporting the truth on television, and Frank departs to investigate the waves. Meanwhile, Redgate and Betty visit the National Bubble Chemical Company and meet company head W. I. Norton Donovan (played by Joe Negri) asking about spray sweaters. Donovan angrily tells them that "we pay you to sell it on television, not to ask questions about it". Betty accuses Donovan of fraud, and points out that the air from the cans will make the windstorm even worse. After Betty and Redgate leave, Donovan reveals his true identity; he is the Wind (a fact foreshadowed by Donovan's four initials). He changes into his true form and flies off to wreak havoc.

Back at the dock, the winds and waves worsen, and the captain and vendor watch on the news as Redgate warns citizens not to use the spray cans; but he is too late. The news team apologizes to Hildegarde Hummingbird and begs her to come back and save Bubbleland. After some deliberation, she agrees, telling them she is on her way and that they should build a wall in the meantime. Everyone gathers at the docks and constructs a wall out of banana crates to keep out the waves and the wind, and Betty quickly knits a giant sweater to cover it all. The Wind arrives, doing his worst, but Hildegarde is there to stop him. After an epic battle, Hildegarde forces the wind to retreat, and Bubbleland is saved. When the danger is past, Hildegarde appears to be dead and a sad moment and song follows, until everyone realizes she has survived after all.

Windstorm in Bubbleland demonstrates just how different Rogers' show can be. Corporate greed, impending natural disaster, and the media cover-up of both (and all in the form of an opera) is a far cry from the kind of content found on most children's programming (and in 1980, at that). Through careful consideration of how children view the world, Rogers is able to introduce almost any topic by carefully interpreting it for children, reshaping the message to fit their understanding. This stands in contrast to children's shows which exploit certain tendencies of children, including consumerist ones, especially when the shows merchandise their characters and turn them into series of character-related toys. Even PBS shows, which do not include advertisements, can still play on the effectiveness of the television commercial format. According to *Sesame Street* writer Emily Kingsley,

> I think the philosophy of *Sesame Street* in terms of teaching was this notion that kids were very responsive to commercials, that they like their information short and sweet and compact, that the attention span, you know, is variable, and that ... the whole concept of today's *Sesame Street* was brought to you by the letter "A" and the letter "B"—the basic commercial that is brought to you by Ivory Soap.[100]

Rogers' show helped children to develop an understanding of the meaning of learning itself, so as to increase their desire to learn. According to Hedda Sharapan (director of special projects and associate producer of *Mister Rogers' Neighborhood*),

> I once heard Fred say—one thing is giving children the facts of education, the other is giving them the tools of education. If we give them the tools of education they will want to learn the facts, and they will use the facts ... to build and not destroy because the question is not will they learn the facts. The question is what will they do with the facts they've learned. So what are the tools of education? Things like feeling good about yourself, being able to handle your relationship with authority figures, with your peers, curiosity, play, those kinds of things, knowing that you can express and control your feelings, you can find healthy outlets for them.[101]

And to be able to use the tools of education, children must have a sense of security, of knowing that they can flourish in the environment they are in. This involves the emotional stability of a supportive family, which encourages success without causing undue fear of failure, in which a child can express themselves and be listened to and appreciated for who they are. As Rogers said,

> It's one of the important parts of the Neighborhood, knowing that feelings are all right. You know, that you don't have to hide them and that there are ways that you can say how you feel that aren't going to hurt you or anybody else. If there was a legacy that I

would hope for the Neighborhood passing on, that's certainly one of them.[102]

Fred Rogers left an enormous legacy, a result not only of his television programs and imaginary world, but also of other appearances and projects on which he worked during and after the run of *Mister Rogers' Neighborhood*, and this is the topic of the final chapter of this book.

6 Mister Rogers' Legacy

Somebody stopped me on the street today and she just said, "You do good work." I said, "Oh, thank you for saying that." Then she said, "Who are you mentoring?" I said, "We have lots of grand people on the Neighborhood, but I sure wish that more programs were fashioning themselves the way we have learned to fashion ourselves for children because I don't see a lot of replication of our kind of work."
Fred Rogers[103]

As evidenced by various awards and recognitions, including four Emmy Awards, a Peabody Award in 1968, the Presidential Medal of Freedom in 2002, a congressional resolution (#111), a star on Hollywood's Walk of Fame in 1998, a cameo appearance as "Reverend Thomas" in episode 19, season 4 of *Dr. Quinn, Medicine Woman* (1993–8), and even an asteroid (26858 Misterrogers) named after him, Fred Rogers arguably achieved cult status, but one which was never self-serving and was unlike those of other late twentieth century celebrities. Likewise, his show has become one of the longest-running children's shows on PBS, and continues in syndication.

When Fred Rogers retired in 2001, no one could have taken over as host of the show; as the show's writer, the voice of many of the Neighborhood of Make-Believe's puppets, and composer of much of the show's music, Rogers' departure left a gap that could not be filled. The show remains in syndication for yet another generation, however, and Rogers' legacy continues to grow, even after his death in 2003 from stomach cancer. And his legacy also includes a number of other projects during the years he created his television show and afterward.

Projects Concurrent with *Mister Rogers' Neighborhood*

In 1967, before his program became broadcast nationally, Rogers was already a celebrity and the subject of the documentary *Creative Person: Fred Rogers* (1967) made by MatchGame Productions. It begins with crowds of parents and children waiting in line in the rain, and a voiceover which says,

> They stand in long lines; children around the country stand for hours, regardless of cold rain, patient beyond the patience of childhood, to see him. They do it because they love him; because he is Fred Rogers, minister, educator, television producer, and, above all, Mister Rogers of *MisteRoger's Neighborhood*.[104]

The film shows him at work on his show and his work as a consultant at the University of Pittsburgh Child Study Center, and describes his work with children in both.

In addition to his regular television show, Rogers made a number of specials over the years which used the same sets and cast as his show, including three "Let's Talk about" specials (*Let's Talk about Wearing a Cast* (1976), *Let's Talk about Having an Operation* (1976), and *Let's Talk about Going to the Hospital* (1976), each of which had a supplemental book published along with it); the hour-long specials *Christmastime with Mister Rogers* (1977), *Mister Rogers Talks with Parents about School* (1979), and *Mister Rogers Talks with Parents about Divorce* (1981); and discussion-oriented programs for adults, including *Mister Rogers Talks with Parents about Competition* (1981), *Mister Rogers Talks with Parents about Pets* (1982), *Mister Rogers Talks with Parents about Make-Believe* (1982), and *Mister Rogers Talks with Parents about Daycare* (1983).

Besides testifying before Congress in 1969, Rogers also testified again during the court case *Sony Corp. of America* v. *Universal City Studios, Inc.* (argued in 1983 and decided in 1984). When commercial VCRs became available in 1976, Universal Pictures and Walt Disney Productions took Sony to court to halt the sales of Betamax recorders, claiming that the recording of television programs was copyright infringement. Though the court ruled in favor of Sony, Universal appealed in 1981 and had the ruling reversed. Sony appealed, and in the resulting case, Rogers testified in favor of allowing VCRs and the taping of programs, stating,

> Some public stations, as well as commercial stations, program the Neighborhood at hours when some children cannot use it. I think that it's a real service to families to be able to record such programs and show them at appropriate times. I have always felt that with the advent of all of this new technology that allows people to tape the Neighborhood off-the-air, and I'm speaking for the Neighborhood because that's what I produce, that they then become much more active in the programming of their family's television life. Very frankly, I am opposed to people being programmed by others. My whole approach in broadcasting has always been "You are an important person just the way you are. You can make healthy decisions." Maybe I'm going on too long, but I just feel that anything that allows a person to be more active in the control of his or her life, in a healthy way, is important.[105]

Thanks in part to Rogers' testimony, the court ruled in favor of Sony again, assuring the rights of consumers to record programs, and also providing a precedent for future intellectual property cases in the years ahead.

Rogers also had intellectual property of his own besides his show, with the publication of several books, including *Mister Rogers Talks to Parents* (1983, co-authored with Barry Head), and, later, *You Are Special: Words of Wisdom for All Ages from a Beloved Neighbor* (1995), *Dear Mister Rogers, Does It Ever Rain in Your Neighborhood? Letters to Mister Rogers* (1996), and *The Mister Rogers Parenting Book: Helping to Understand Your Young Child* (2002). He also made several record albums of his songs, including *Let's Be Together Today* (1968) and *Won't You Be My Neighbor* (1973), both of which were re-released multiple times and mentioned and shown on his program (see Figure 6.1). (The year 2005 would even see *Songs From the Neighborhood: The Music of Mister Rogers*, an album of cover versions of Rogers' songs done by contemporary artists.) Toys, books, cassettes, and other merchandise based on *Mister Rogers' Neighborhood* were also released over the years (like Small World Enterprise's *Neighbor of Make-Believe Playset* from 1970), but nowhere near the extent to

Figure 6.1 Rogers holding his record albums in episodes 0078 (top, left), 0091 (top, right), and 1006 (bottom, left); and a record album rack full of Rogers' albums at Negri's Music Shop in episode 1488 (bottom, right; the album rack is on the left side of the image).

which other children's programs like *Sesame Street* were merchandising their worlds, characters, and franchises.

Rogers' main interest was education, and his lifelong fascination with the sky and astronomy led him to obtain a pilot's license while still in high school; he later developed a planetarium show, *The Sky above Mister Rogers' Neighborhood* (2001), which is still shown in planetariums. Rogers also brought his messages about children to his public appearances, as a guest on *The Tonight Show* (July 7, 1983, and April 29, 1986, both guest hosted by Joan Rivers), *The Arsenio Hall Show* in 1993, and *The Rosie O'Donnell Show* in 1996. He even brought some of his puppets on the show, voicing them in front of the audience.

Some projects involved transmedial adaptations of the Neighborhood of Make-Believe. In the late 1980s, Rogers did the voices for and was involved in the design of the Neighborhood of Make-Believe theme park ride at Idlewild Park just outside Latrobe, Pennsylvania, Rogers' hometown. According to the sign outside the ride,

In designing the ride, Fred Rogers wanted to create an experience using some of the familiar and whimsical elements of "Mister Rogers' Neighborhood." The Neighborhood of Make-Believe was a natural setting for that, and the Trolley where families could ride together was the perfect "vehicle"! It was especially important to him that this ride create an atmosphere that would bring children and their favorite adults together in warm and caring ways—a true extension of the overall philosophy of Mister Rogers' Neighborhood. After developing the story line, he and his production team at Family Communications, Inc., the non-profit company that he founded, worked closely with the team from Idlewild and Kennywood to design the ride which opened the summer of 1989.[106]

For the ride, passengers boarded a full-size trolley, traveled through a tunnel, and passed various neighborhood locations where animatronics versions of Rogers' puppets could be seen moving, as the ride's "tour guide" interacted with recordings of Rogers' voices for the puppets (which had moving mouths and eyes, unlike some of the show's puppets (see Figure 6.2)). Another tunnel ended the ride, returning passengers to the rest of the theme park. (A video of the entire ride can be viewed at http://www.youtube.com/watch?v=hKQRJvw0XEs.)

Other projects that Rogers worked on include a recreation of his television house at the Children's Museum of Pittsburgh and The Fred Rogers Center for Early Learning and Children's Media, at Saint Vincent College. Rogers began working on The Fred Rogers Center in 2000, which continued after his death in February of 2003 before finally opening a few months later in September. According to the Center's website, its mission is "to advance the fields of early learning and children's media by acting as a catalyst for communication, collaboration, and creative change".[107] The international center runs The Fred Rogers Archive; The Fred Rogers Center Fellows Program for senior scholars and for early-career and aspiring professionals in educational children's media; The Fred Rogers Center Early Learning Environment (an on-line community for early learning); and The Fred Forward Conference Series, a three-day annual conference on children's education and entertainment. The Fred Rogers Center, along with Saint Vincent College, with which it is associated, represents the major force carrying on Rogers' work and

Figure 6.2 Animatronics puppets that appeared in the Neighborhood of Make-Believe theme park ride at Idlewild Park: in the front row, King Friday and Queen Sara; in the back row, from left to right, Henrietta Pussycat, X the Owl, Cornflake S. Pecially, Prince Tuesday, Daniel Striped Tiger, Ana Platypus, and Elsie Jean Platypus. Photograph from Wikimedia Commons, "Mr. Rogers Neighborhood at w:Idlewild and Soak Zone", by J. Aaron Farr, August 30, 2008, available in color at http://www.flickr.com/photos/jaaronfarr/2811111557/.

investigation into the relationship between children's television and education.

After the *Neighborhood*

Mister Rogers' Neighborhood finally ceased production in 2001, and after Rogers' death in 2003, much of the material having to do with the show went to The Fred Rogers Archive and Exhibit at The Fred Rogers Center, including the puppets used on the show. Family Communications, Inc., which Rogers founded in 1971 and which produced his program, was renamed The Fred Rogers Company in 2010, and carries on his legacy today.

With several generations of viewers, Rogers influenced children's television, and even public television in general, for example, by his court testimonies as mentioned above. Rogers' effect on the journalists who interviewed him was even the subject of a 2003 study done by Temple University Professor Ronald Bishop, who looked at the work of eighty-three journalists and how they typically began with skepticism and ended up captivated by Rogers' message, setting aside their objectivity and even writing about what effect Rogers had on them personally.[108] Apparently journalists were not the only ones affected; Bishop mentions what happened during Rogers' trip to the Soviet Union, writing,

> As part of a 1987 journey to the former Soviet Union to appear on a children's television program (Brennan, Margulies, & Baker, 1988, p. 7-D; Allen, 1987, p. B-1; Barringer, 1987, p. 10), Rogers said he hoped to "build a little bridge on behalf of children" (Brennan, Margulies, & Baker, p. 7-D). Negotiations about his appearance stalled until Rogers turned for help to Daniel Striped Tiger, a puppet well known to Neighborhood viewers. "They just lit up", Rogers recalled about Daniel's greeting to the Soviet negotiators (Barringer, 1987, p. 10).[109]

Roger's co-workers were also inspired to carry on his work. Perhaps the best example is David Newell, who is Director of Public Relations at The Fred Rogers Company and who continues to make appearances as Mr. McFeely. Documentary filmmaker Paul Germain even made a feature-length film about Newell, *Speedy Delivery* (2008), which shows him going about his work, as himself and as Mr. McFeely. Other documentaries have also appeared, like the Emmy-nominated *Fred Rogers: America's Favorite Neighbor* (2004), and *Mister Rogers & Me: A Deep & Simple Documentary Film* (2010) by MTV news producer Benjamin Wagner, who came to know Rogers when his mother rented a cottage next door to Rogers' summer home in Nantucket. A number of books by people who knew Rogers, like Tim Madigan's *I'm Proud of You: My Friendship with Fred Rogers* (2006) and Amy Hollingsworth's *The Simple Faith of Mister Rogers: Spiritual Insights from the World's Most Beloved Neighbor* (2007), also recount experiences of people whose lives he touched, providing further anecdotes about Rogers and giving more insight into the man.

Dozens of post-hiatus episodes of *Mister Rogers' Neighborhood* can be watched on-line at PBS's website (http://pbskids.org/rogers/), and even some pre-hiatus episodes are available for purchase on-line. Footage of Rogers and his show circulates on the Internet as well, and is sometimes reappropriated or imitated. Some of it is inevitably parody, such as sound clips of Rogers used to make prank phone calls, and parody segments from National Lampoon ("Mister Robert's Neighborhood") (1970–98), *Saturday Night Live* (Eddie Murphy's "Mister Robinson's Neighborhood" (1975–present), about a dangerous inner-city neighborhood), *MAD* Magazine (1952–present), *Robot Chicken* (2005–present), Tom Wilson's *Ziggy* (1968–present), *Family Guy* (1990–present), and others. But some material is also homage; for example, on June 7, 2012, PBS Digital Studios posted on-line an autotuned music video, "Garden of Your Mind", edited from *Mister Rogers' Neighborhood* video and sound clips by John D. Boswell (a.k.a. melodysheep). It quickly went viral and received a million views per day in its first few days on-line. The video sets Rogers' voice to music and has images edited to match, resulting in a music video about curiosity and imagination.

In 2006, Family Communications contacted Angela Santomero, creator of the children's program *Blue's Clues* (1996–2006), to work on a spinoff television series based on characters from the Neighborhood of Make-Believe. The result was the animated program *Daniel Tiger's Neighborhood*, which debuted on September 3, 2012. The show's main characters are descendants of the characters from the original show; Daniel Tiger is the son of Daniel Striped Tiger, is grown up, and now works at the clock factory located in the clock that was once his home. Katerina Kittycat is Henrietta Pussycat's daughter, and O the Owl is X the Owl's nephew. Prince Wednesday is the son of King Friday and younger brother of Prince Tuesday, and Miss Elaina is the daughter of Lady Elaine Fairchilde and Music Man Stan.

Even though the original Neighborhood characters are more or less in the background, some of them have been changed, without explanation. King Friday has lost much of his pomposity, Queen Sara has lost her southern accent, and Lady Elaine's character has been whitewashed and made over; though intended as a link to the earlier program, these characters no longer have the unique personalities that made them stand out in the original series. Lady Elaine doesn't even look the same, and her new, redesigned character is fairly bland by comparison, eliminating some of the diversity found on Rogers' original show. Fan and blogger Brigid K. Barjaktarevic articulated her disgust with the changes, writing,

> My one complaint about the show is that Lady Elaine Fairchilde is historically pretty ugly. She had a big nose and chin and

terrible hair and a frumpy red dress. In the cartoon, she's slender and attractive with a stylish hair cut. I loved ugly Lady Elaine Fairchilde and am disappointed she's been given a make over. Less-than-beautiful people on tv make me feel better about my own less-than-beautiful bits.[110]

It is somewhat ironic, and perhaps an indication of how far the current program has strayed from Rogers' original philosophy, that one of Rogers' most repeated messages, "People can like you just the way you are", has been violated so blatantly. One might even argue that the whole point of Lady Elaine's looks and behavior was used for lessons about getting along and liking others, regardless of looks and in spite of their behavior.

Daniel Tiger's Neighborhood is far more conventional a program than Rogers' show was, taking fewer risks and lacking the whimsy and multiple levels of meanings in references that only an adult would get (for example, literary references). Yet while such differences may underscore Rogers' originality and genius when it came to developing children's programming, the show is still a popular one and has found great success with its intended audience, getting the third-highest rating for the 2–5 age group after its premiere and making Nielsen's top ten list of shows favored by mothers 18–49 with children under the age of three.[111]

The unique outlook and blend of elements of *Mister Rogers' Neighborhood* has never been duplicated, and probably never will. Sweet without being saccharine, simple without being dumbed-down or pandering, and designed to be watched by children together with their parents, the show embodied Rogers' deep understanding of children and of human nature in general. The show's themes and messages still apply today, allowing the show to remain relevant, and it will probably continue to do so, well into the future. We are not likely to find another show or host like Rogers, and hopefully his program will remain available to future generations of children (and parents) for years to come.

List of Episodes

Of the program's 895 episodes, 590 were produced during the period 1968–76, with the remaining 305 episodes produced 1979–2001, after a three-year hiatus. The 590 earlier episodes are no longer shown on television, though some of them are now available on video. Listed below are the 305 post-hiatus episodes, most of which are still shown in syndication. Five half-hour episodes were made for each topic, and were designed to be seen daily Monday through Friday in a single week, with storylines in the Neighborhood of Make-Believe (and occasionally in the television home segments) running through all five episodes.

Episodes	Year
0001–0130	1968
1001–1065	1969
1066–1130	1970
1131–1195	1971
1196–1260	1972
1261–1325	1973
1326–1390	1974
1391–1455	1975
1456–1460	1976

Episodes	Original Air Date	Topic
1461–1465	(August 20–24, 1979)	Goes to School
1466–1470	(February 4–8, 1980)	Superheroes
1471–1475	(May 19–23, 1980)	Makes an Opera (Windstorm in Bubbleland)
1476–1480	(February 16–20, 1981)	Divorce
1481–1485	(June 1–5, 1981)	Competition
1486–1490	(July 20–24, 1981)	Play
1491–1495	(March 1–5, 1982)	Discipline
1496–1500	(May 31–June 4, 1982)	Pets
1501–1505	(June 28–July 2, 1982)	Make-Believe
1506–1510	(November 15–19, 1982)	Friends
1511–1515	(February 7–11, 1983)	Games
1516–1520	(April 25–29, 1983)	Day and Night Care
1521–1525	(November 7–11, 1983)	Conflict
1526–1530	(April 2–6, 1984)	Work
1531–1535	(May 7–11, 1984)	Grandparents
1536–1540	(November 19–23, 1984)	Food
1541–1545	(February 4–8, 1985)	No & Yes
1546–1550	(May 13–17, 1985)	Music
1551–1555	(November 25–29, 1985)	Families
1556–1560	(February 3–7, 1986)	Making & Creating
1561–1565	(May 5–9, 1986)	Celebrations
1566–1570	(November 24–28, 1986)	Playthings
1571–1575	(March 7–11, 1987)	Dance
1576–1580	(May 4–8, 1987)	Making Mistakes
1581–1585	(November 23–27, 1987)	Alike and Different
1586–1590	(March 7–11, 1988)	Nighttime
1591–1595	(May 2–6, 1988)	Kindness and Unkindness
1596–1600	(November 21–25, 1988)	Secrets
1601–1605	(February 20–24, 1989)	Fun & Games
1606–1610	(May 1–5, 1989)	Josephine the Short-Neck Giraffe
1611–1615	(November 20–24, 1989)	When Parents Go To Work
1616–1620	(April 16–20, 1990)	The Environment
1621–1625	(July 30–August 3, 1990)	Fathers and Music
1626–1630	(November 19–23, 1990)	Mouths and Feelings
1631–1635	(February 25–March 1, 1991)	Growing
1636–1640	(August 27–31, 1991)	Dress-Up
1641–1645	(November 25–29, 1991)	Art
1646–1650	(February 24–28, 1992)	Imaginary Friends
1651–1655	(August 24–28, 1992)	Learning
1656–1660	(November 23–27, 1992)	Up & Down
1661–1665	(February 22–26, 1993)	Love

Notes

1 Fred Rogers, during an interview with CNN, as quoted in "Fred Rogers", PBS: Pioneers of Television, 2014, http://www.pbs.org/opb/pioneersoftelevision/pioneering-people/fred-rogers/.
2 David McCullough, quoted at Nancy E. Curry, "Designed for Children: The Groundbreaking Approach of the *Neighborhood*", The Fred Rogers Center, n.d., http://exhibit.fredrogerscenter.org/groundbreaking-work/designed-for-children.
3 Lucille Burbank, *Children's Television: An Historical Inquiry on Three Selected, Prominent, Long-running Early Childhood TV Programs*, Doctoral Dissertation, Temple University, 1992. Although Keeshan stated in an interview with Burbank that the show's purpose was to educate and entertain children under the age of eight and build a child's self-esteem, with more attention paid to emotional development than intellectual development, the show's producer, Sam Gibbon, said the show was "not an educational program; it was an entertainment program" (Burbank, page 84), and the show's puppeteer Gus Allegretti also felt it was not educational (Burbank, page 126).
4 Ibid., pages 87 and 116.
5 Ibid., page 221.
6 Ibid., page 217.
7 Ibid., page 218.
8 L. K. Friedrich and A. H. Stein, *Aggressive and Prosocial Television Programs and the Natural Behavior of Preschool Children*, Monographs of the Society for the Research in Child Development 38(4), 1973, page 45.
9 Joan Ganz Cooney begins her foreword to *"G" is for Growing: Thirty Years of Research on Children and Sesame Street* by writing, "Without research, there would be no Sesame Street. For all its obviousness now, the notion of combining research with television production was positively heretical in 1967 when we first began making plans for the Children's Television Workshop (CTW) and what would eventually become, in fact, the most researched television show in history" (Shalom M. Fisch and Rosemary T. Truglio, editors, *"G" is for Growing: Thirty Years of Research on Children and Sesame Street*, Mahwah, NJ: Lawrence Erlbaum Associates, 2001, page xi).

10 Ibid., page 219.
11 Rogers received many letters and would sometimes use suggestions and ideas for themes on the shows, so if the week-long storylines had received any complaints, chances are that they would have been changed. However, there is no evidence that anyone found them too confusing to follow. Examples of continuing narratives involving the television home segments include the week (episodes 1496–1500) when Rogers took care of Bob Trow's dog, Barney, and the week (episodes 1586–1590) involving visits to and from Russian children's TV host Tatiana Vedeneeva.
12 According to Sam Gibbon, writer and associate producer of *Captain Kangaroo*; see Burbank, page 135.
13 Burbank, *Children's Television*, page 288. Burbank also gives the figure of $3,600 per episode for *Captain Kangaroo* in 1955.
14 Paul B. Brown and Maria Fisher, "Big Bird Cashes In", *Forbes*, November 5, 1984, page 178.
15 As quoted in John Kiesewetter, "A Day in Mister Rogers' Neighborhood", *Cincinnati Enquirer*, November 11, 1997, available at http://www.enquirer.com/editions/1997/11/17/loc_rogers.html.
16 Fred Rogers and Barry Head, *Mister Rogers Talks to Parents*, Pittsburgh, Pennsylvania: Family Communications, Inc., 1983, page 48.
17 Amy Hollingsworth, *The Simple Faith of Mister Rogers: Spiritual Insights from the World's Most Beloved Neighbor*, Nashville, Tennessee: Thomas Nelson, Inc., 2005, page 1.
18 According to Betty Aberlin; see Bill Madison and Betty Aberlin, "Interview: Betty Aberlin", *Billevesées: Fiction, Non-fiction, and Nonsense from an American in Paris (Sometimes)*, March 22, 2009, available at http://billmadison.blogspot.com/2009/03/interview-betty-aberlin.html.
19 Fred Rogers, *Dear Mister Rogers, Does It Ever Rain in Your Neighborhood? Letters to Mister Rogers*, New York: Penguin Books, 1996, pages 36–37.
20 Burbank, *Children's Television*, page 161.
21 George Romero, "Bloody Diary, Part 2", *The Official DiamondDead Website*, 2004-01-15, 14:38:11, available at http://web.archive.org/web/20070216005517/http://www.diamonddead.com/diary/view.php?s=YToyOntzOjM6ImFpZCI7czoxOiIzIjtzOjI6ImlkIjtzOjI6IjI4Ijt9. Romero wanted to cast Betty Aberlin as the lead in *Night of the Living Dead* (1968), but Rogers apparently refused. Rogers saw Romero's first two *Dead* movies, and thought them "a lot of fun", according to Peter Hartlaub ("'Dead' and Fred: George A. Romero's connection to Mr. Rogers", May 13, 2009, available at http://blog.sfgate.com/parenting/2010/05/13/dead-and-fred-george-a-romeros-connection-to-mr-rogers/). Don Brockett would later go on to play a zombie in Romero's *Day of the Dead* (1985), and Brockett, Chuck Aber, and Romero would all have bit parts in *The Silence of the Lambs* (1991).
22 Rogers, *Dear Mister Rogers*, page 41.
23 Ibid., page 40.
24 Hollingsworth, *The Simple Faith of Mister Rogers*, page 19.

25 For examples of interesting moments of dialogue that appear to be ad-libbed on camera, see the description of episode 1361 at http://www.neighborhoodarchive.com/mrn/episodes/1361/index.html.

26 Robert Bianco, "The Quiet Success of Fred Rogers", *Pittsburgh Press Sunday Magazine*, March 26, 1989, page 22.

27 Burbank, *Children's Television*, page 46, citing M. L. Polak, "Fred Rogers: An Honest Adult", *The Philadelphia Enquirer*, December 9, 1984, page 17.

28 Hollingsworth, *The Simple Faith of Mister Rogers*, page 60.

29 Jerome L. Singer and Dorothy G. Singer, *Television, Imagination, and Aggression: A Study of Preschoolers*, Hillsdale, NJ: Lawrence Erlbaum Associates, 1981, page 4.

30 Ibid., page 6.

31 Fred B. Rainsberry, *A History of Children's Television in English Canada, 1952–1986*, New Jersey: Metuchen, 1988, page 188.

32 As quoted in Hollingworth, *The Simple Faith of Mister Rogers*, page xxii.

33 The story is recounted in Benjamin Wagner's film *Mister Rogers & Me* (2010), as well as in Hollingsworth, *The Simple Faith of Mister Rogers*, pages 125–6.

34 Rogers, *Dear Mister Rogers*, page 24.

35 Burbank, *Children's Television*, page 166.

36 Rogers and Head, *Mister Rogers Talks to Parents*, page 162.

37 Margaret Mary Kimmel and Mark Collins, *The Wonder of It All: Fred Rogers and the Story of an Icon*, Latrobe, PA: The Fred Rogers Center at St. Vincent's College, 2008, page 11.

38 Burbank, *Children's Television*, page 139.

39 Rogers and Head, *Mister Rogers Talks to Parents*, page 163.

40 Burbank, *Children's Television*, pages 154–5.

41 Ibid., page 39. For the figures, Burbank cites G. H. Grossman, *Saturday Morning TV*, New York: Dell, 1981.

42 Ibid., page 148.

43 Ibid., page 139.

44 Ibid., page 164.

45 Ibid., page 164.

46 The study was Freidrich and Stein, 1973, and the quote comes from Singer and Singer, 1981, page 10.

47 Ibid., page 140.

48 Kimmel and Collins, *The Wonder of It All: Fred Rogers and the Story of an Icon*, pages 14–15. The first quote comes from Fred Rogers, Archive Interview for the Archive of American Television, conducted by Karen Herman on July 22, 1999, available at http://www.emmytvlegends.org/interviews/people/fred-rogers, page 57. The web blogger's quote is from *Television Transcript Project*, Mister Rogers #1614, available at http://www.geocities.com/tvtranscripts/mrrogers/mr_1614.htm.

49 Donald Horton and R. Richard Wohl, "Mass Communication and Para-Social Interaction: Observations on Intimacy at a Distance", *Psychiatry* 19(3), 1956, pages 215–29, and reprinted in *Particip@tions*, 3(1), May 2006.

50 Aaron Gell, "The Crimes of Mister Rogers: He Meow-Meow Lied to Us Meow", *New York Observer*, March 19, 2012, available at http://observer. com/2012/03/the-crimes-of-mister-rogers-he-meow-meow-lied-to-us-meow/#ixzz2l1dk0PLl.

51 Samples of letters from these viewers can be found in Rogers, *Dear Mister Rogers*.

52 Ibid., pages 6–8.

53 In episode 1006, Rogers gives directions from the front door of his television house to King Friday's Castle, saying, "Right down the street to the second block and then to the right ... after that you'll see Make-Believe", but such a connection is arguably non-canonical. (Thanks to Tim Lybrager and the Neighborhood Archive for this information.)

54 While most writers understandably spell Cornflake S. Pecially's nickname "Corny", this is incorrect, as Rogers himself spells it "Corney" (probably because the character's name was originally "Cornelius"). See for example Rogers and Head, *Mister Rogers Talks to Parents*, page 167.

55 I can remember being very young and watching the show and finding such spatial relationships fascinating.

56 In *Daniel Tiger's Neighborhood*, Daniel Striped Tiger is Daniel's father, and his wife is referred to only as "Mom Tiger". Assuming the two series are consistent, either she is the same as Collette (they do not look alike, but this is also true of other versions of characters bridging the two series), or Daniel has been (or will be) married more than once, or the crystal ball is wrong.

57 See Tom Junod, "Pittsburgh in Words – Can you say 'Hero'?", *Esquire*, 130(5), November 1998, available at http://urie.us/mr-rogers.html. The number 143 was originally assigned to Minot's Ledge Lighthouse in 1894 as its distinctive signal; see http://lighthouse.cc/minots/index.html. (Thanks to Tim Lybrager and the Neighborhood Archive for this information.)

58 See Roger's 1993 appearance on *The Arsenio Hall Show*, and Kimmel and Collins, pages 7–8.

59 Burbank, *Children's Television*, page 212.

60 Ibid., pages 248–9.

61 As demonstrated in Nina E. Lerman, Ruth Oldenziel, and Arwen P. Mohun, "Introduction: Interrogating Boundaries", in Nina E. Lerman, Ruth Oldenziel, and Arwen P. Mohun, editors, *Gender & Technology: A Reader*, Baltimore, MD: Johns Hopkins University Press, 2003, pages 1–2.

62 Aram Bakshian, Jr., "Gone with the Wimp", *National Review*, 37(18), September 20, 1985, page 49.

63 Even the minor roles in scenes of the real neighborhood were racially diverse; for example, both the court clerk and the judge are black in episode 1210, where Rogers goes to court to argue against a parking ticket he had received. Many black people are also present at the McFeelys' wedding, which, since it is set in 1936, shows them to be ahead of their time when it comes to race relations.

64 The character of Music Man Stan appears to have been based on the "Music Man" character, a black man with an afro and sideburns played by Stanley Clay on the 1977 special "Christmastime with Mister Rogers";

but according to Brittany Smith of The Fred Rogers Company, Music Man Stan from *Daniel Tiger's Neighborhood* was not based on the character played by Stanley Clay. The reader, however, is invited to compare the animated character (http://www.neighborhoodarchive.com/dtn/characters/music_man_stan/index.html) and the live-action character (http://www.neighborhoodarchive.com/video/other/christmastime/index.html) and note the similarities.

65 According to Betty Aberlin; see Madison and Aberlin.

66 I can remember being four years old and watching the show and finding his liminality disturbing (yet fascinating) even then, since he was such an even combination of human and canine features.

67 In very early episodes, while the show's ontological rules were still forming, there are occasionally exceptions, like Betty Aberlin appearing in the television house as Lady Aberlin in episode 0038, Joe Negri appearing the television house as Handyman Negri in episodes 1002 and 1020, and Officer Clemmons appearing in both the television house and the Neighborhood of Make-Believe in episodes 1012 and 1018. Many guest stars also appear in the television neighborhood as well as the Neighborhood of Make-Believe.

68 Going a step further, in *A Granddad for Daniel*, the opera performed in episode 1535, a human salesman (played by John Reardon) decides to marry a starfish (played by Betty Okonak Templeton Jones).

69 Burbank, *Children's Television*, page 102.

70 See http://muppet.wikia.com/wiki/Mister_Rogers'_Neighborhood.

71 From writings sent by Rogers in response to a child's letter; see Rogers, *Dear Mister Rogers*, page 94.

72 Kimmel and Collins, *The Wonder of It All*, page 3.

73 Donna Mitroff and Rebecca Herr Stephenson, "The Television Tug-of-War: A Brief History of Children's Television Programming in the United States", in J. Alison Bryant, editor, *The Children's Television Community*, Mahwah, NJ: Lawrence Erlbaum Associates, 2006, pages 24–5.

74 J. M. Laskas, "The Gospel According to Fred Rogers", *The Philadelphia Inquirer Magazine*, November 22, 1987, page 38.

75 Rogers and Head, *Mister Rogers Talks to Parents*, page 164.

76 Burbank, *Children's Television*, page 176.

77 Ibid., page 187.

78 Jeffrey Zaslow, "Blame It on Mr. Rogers: Why Young Adults Feel So Entitled", *The Wall Street Journal*, July 5, 2007, available at http://online.wsj.com/news/articles/SB118358476840657463.

79 Rogers, *Dear Mister Rogers*, pages xii–xiii.

80 Don Chance, "Rants & Raves: Mr. Rogers and the Entitlement Generation", available at http://www.bus.lsu.edu/academics/finance/faculty/dchance/Rants&Raves_Mr_Rogers_and_the_Entitlement_Generation.htm.

81 Ibid.

82 Richard Lee Colvin, "Losing Faith in Self-Esteem Movement", *Los Angeles Times*, January 25, 1999, available at http://articles.latimes.com/1999/jan/25/news/mn-1505.

83 The monastery, Saint Vincent Archabbey, was in his hometown of Latrobe, Pennsylvania; and the center named after Rogers is at Saint Vincent's College. The church which Rogers attended while summering in Nantucket, St. Paul's Episcopal, is shown in the Wagner Brothers' film *Mister Rogers & Me* (2010).

84 As Rogers admitted in a quote found in Hollingworth, *The Simple Faith of Mister Rogers*, page 137.

85 The song can be found at http://www.youtube.com/watch?v=j9FXoH_JvZ8. Occasionally one could find other direct references in children's programming; for example, on *Romper Room* (1953–94), a prayer was said before the children ate.

86 Bakshian, page 50.

87 Hollingworth, *The Simple Faith of Mister Rogers*, page 10.

88 The speech can be seen at http://www.youtube.com/watch?v=Upm9LnuC BUM&NR=1&feature=endscreen.

89 Hollingsworth, *The Simple Faith of Mister Rogers*, page 7. Her quotation of Rogers comes from Rev. Gordon McClellan, "Interview: Fred Rogers", *Christian Networks Journal*, June 2001.

90 For example, Amy Hollingsworth, Tim Madigan, and Benjamin Wagner.

91 Hollingworth, *The Simple Faith of Mister Rogers*, pages 160–1.

92 Madison and Aberlin.

93 Burbank, *Children's Television*, page 204.

94 Gerald S. Lesser and Joel Schneider, "Creation and Evolution of the *Sesame Street* Curriculum", in Shalom M. Fisch and, Rosemary T. Truglio, editors, *"G" is for Growing: Thirty Years of Research on Children and Sesame Street*, Mahwah, NJ: Lawrence Erlbaum Associates, 2001, pages 31–5.

95 From Rogers' testimony before Senator Pastore and the US Senate Subcommittee on Communication in 1969. His testimony can be viewed at http://www.youtube.com/watch?v=yXEuEUQIP3Q.

96 Kiesewetter.

97 Hollingsworth, *The Simple Faith of Mister Rogers*, page 119.

98 Henri Matisse as quoted in C. J. Bulliet, *The Significant Moderns and Their Pictures*, New York: Halcyon House, 1936, page 46.

99 From Part 2 of the Fred Rogers Archive Interview for the Archive of American Television conducted by Karen Herman on July 22, 1999, available at http://www.emmytvlegends.org/interviews/people/fred-rogers.

100 Burbank, *Children's Television*, page 214.

101 Ibid., page 187.

102 Fred Rogers, as quoted in Hollingsworth, *The Simple Faith of Mister Rogers*, pages 61–2.

103 As quoted in Burbank, *Children's Television*, page 181.

104 The documentary can be seen at http://www.youtube.com/watch?v=NSC qkfI5t1U (accessed April 4, 2013).

105 See the Home Recording Rights Coalition webpage, available at http:// www.hrrc.org/index.php?id=289&subid=277.

106 The text on the sign, and the ride itself, is described and shown at http:// neighborhoodarchive.com/misc/other/idlewild/.

107 The Fred Rogers Center for Early Learning and Children's Media website, available at http://www.fredrogerscenter.org/about/mission-statement/.

108 Ronald Bishop, "The World's Nicest Grown-Up: A Fantasy Theme Analysis of News Media Coverage of Fred Rogers", *Journal of Communication*, 53(1), 2003, pages 16–31.

109 Ibid., page 18.

110 Brigid K. Barjaktarevic, "Daniel Tiger's Neighborhood", *Now Showing!*, September 3, 2012, http://brigidkeely.com/baby/2012/09/03/daniel-tigers-neighborhood/.

111 According to Dan Sarto, "*Daniel Tiger's Neighborhood* Reaps Rising Ratings", *Animation World Network*, December 3, 2012, available at http://www.awn.com/news/television/daniel-tiger-rises-ratings.

References

Bakshian, Aram Jr., "Gone with the Wimp", *National Review*, 37(18), September 20, 1985, pages 49–50.

Bishop, Ronald, "The World's Nicest Grown-Up: A Fantasy Theme Analysis of News Media Coverage of Fred Rogers", *Journal of Communication*, 53(1), 2003, pages 16–31.

Bulliet, C. J., *The Significant Moderns and Their Pictures*, New York: Halcyon House, 1936.

Burbank, Lucille, *Children's Television: An Historical Inquiry on Three Selected, Prominent, Long-running Early Childhood TV Programs*, Doctoral Dissertation, Temple University, 1992.

Chance, Don, "Rants & Raves: Mr. Rogers and the Entitlement Generation", available at http://www.bus.lsu.edu/academics/finance/faculty/dchance/Rants&Raves_Mr_Rogers_and_the_Entitlement_Generation.htm.

Collins, Mark, and Margaret Mary Kimmel, editors, *Children, Television, and Fred Rogers*, Pittsburgh, PA: University of Pittsburgh Press, 1997.

The Fred Rogers Company (formerly Family Communications) website, available at http://www.fredrogers.org/.

Fisch, Shalom M., and Truglio, Rosemary T., editors, *"G" is for Growing: Thirty Years of Research on Children and Sesame Street*, Mahwah, NJ: Lawrence Erlbaum Associates, 2001.

Friedrich, L. K., and A. H. Stein, "Aggressive and Prosocial Television Programs and the Natural Behavior of Preschool Children", *Monographs of the Society for the Research in Child Development*, 38(4), 1973, pages 1–64.

Gell, Aaron, "The Crimes of Mister Rogers: He Meow-Meow Lied to Us Meow", *New York Observer*, March 19, 2012, available at http://observer.com/2012/03/the-crimes-of-mister-rogers-he-meow-meow-lied-to-us-meow/#ixzz2l1dk0PLl.

Germain, Paul (director), *Speedy Delivery: The Movie*, USA: Speedyfan Productions, 2008.

Grossman, G. H., *Saturday Morning TV*, New York: Dell, 1981.

Hartlaub, Peter, "'Dead' and Fred: George A. Romero's connection to Mr. Rogers", May 13, 2009, available at http://blog.sfgate.com/parenting/2010/05/13/dead-and-fred-george-a-romeros-connection-to-mr-rogers/.

Hollingsworth, Amy, *The Simple Faith of Mister Rogers: Spiritual Insights from the World's Most Beloved Neighbor*, Nashville, TN: Thomas Nelson Publishers, 2007.

Horton, Donald, and R. Richard Wohl, "Mass Communication and Para-Social Interaction: Observations on Intimacy at a Distance", *Psychiatry*, 19(3), 1956, pages 215–29; reprinted in *Particip@tions*, 3(1), May 2006.

Kastelic, Robert, "Mr. Rogers and the Neighborhood as a Model for Understanding Human Behavior", *Skole: The Journal of the National Coalition of Alternative Community Schools*, 15, 1998, pages 92–6.

Kiesewetter, John, "A Day in the Life of Mister Rogers' Neighborhood", *The Cincinnati Enquirer*, November 11, 1997, available at http://www.enquirer.com/editions/1997/11/17/loc_rogers.html.

Kimmel, Margaret Mary, and Mark Collins, *The Wonder of It All: Fred Rogers and the Story of an Icon*, Latrobe, PA: The Fred Rogers Center at St. Vincent's College, 2008, available at http://www.fredrogerscenter.org/media/site_images/Kimmel_and_Collins-pdf_of_pub_version-10-15-08.pdf.

Laskas, J. M., "The Magic of Mister Rogers", USAIR, October 1987.

Madigan, Tim, *I'm Proud of You: My Friendship with Fred Rogers*, Los Angeles, CA: Ubuntu Books, 2006.

Madison, Bill, and Betty Aberlin, "Interview: Betty Aberlin", *Billevesées: Fiction, Non-fiction, and Nonsense from an American in Paris (Sometimes)*, March 22, 2009, available at http://billmadison.blogspot.com/2009/03/interview-betty-aberlin.html.

Mitroff, Donna, and Rebecca Herr Stephenson, "The Television Tug-of-War: A Brief History of Children's Television Programming in the United States", in J. Alison Bryant, editor, *The Children's Television Community*, Mahwah, NJ: Lawrence Erlbaum Associates, 2006, pages 3–34.

Rainsberry, Fred B., *A History of Children's Television in English Canada, 1952–1986*, New Jersey: Metuchen, 1988.

Rogers, Fred, Archive Interview for the Archive of American Television, conducted by Karen Herman on July 22, 1999, available at http://www.emmytvlegends.org/interviews/people/fred-rogers.

Rogers, Fred, *Dear Mister Rogers, Does It Ever Rain in Your Neighborhood? Letters to Mister Rogers*, New York: Penguin Books, 1996.

Rogers, Fred, *The Mister Rogers Parenting Book: Helping to Understand Your Young Child*, Philadelphia, PA: Running Press Book Publishers, 2002.

Rogers, Fred, *You Are Special: Words of Wisdom for All Ages from a Beloved Neighbor*, New York: Penguin, 1995.

Rogers, Fred, and Barry Head, *Mister Rogers Talks to Parents*, Pittsburgh, PA: Family Communications Inc., 1983.

Sarto, Dan, "*Daniel Tiger's Neighborhood* Reaps Rising Ratings", *Animation World Network*, December 3, 2012, available at http://www.awn.com/news/television/daniel-tiger-rises-ratings.

Sebak, Rick (producer), and Patty Walker (director), *Fred Rogers: America's Favorite Neighbor, Parts I and II*, Pittsburgh, PA: Family Communications, Inc., 2003.

Singer, Jerome, and Dorothy Singer, "Come Back, Mister Rogers, Come Back", in Carl Lowe, editor, *Television in American Culture*, New York: Wilson, 1981, pages 124–8.

Singer, Jerome L., and Singer, Dorothy G., *Television, Imagination, and Aggression: A Study of Preschoolers*, Hillsdale, NJ: Lawrence Erlbaum Associates, 1981.

Wagner, Benjamin (director), and Christofer Wagner (film editor), *Mister Rogers & Me*, USA: Wagner Bros., 2010.

Woolery, George W., *Children's Television: The First Thirty-Five Years, 1946–1981*, New York: Scarecrow Press, 1991.

Zaslow, Jeffrey, "Blame It on Mr. Rogers: Why Young Adults Feel So Entitled", *The Wall Street Journal*, July 5, 2007, available at http://online.wsj.com/news/articles/SB118358476840657463.

Index

Printed in the United States
by Baker & Taylor Publisher Services